Personally s[peaking]
Teaching languages for use

Personally speaking...
Teaching languages for use

William Rowlinson

Oxford University Press 1985

Oxford University Press, Walton Street, Oxford OX2 6DP

Oxford London
New York Toronto Melbourne Auckland
Kuala Lumpur Singapore Hong Kong Tokyo
Delhi Bombay Calcutta Madras Karachi
Nairobi Dar es Salaam Cape Town

and associated companies in
Beirut Berlin Ibadan Mexico City Nicosia

Oxford is a trade mark of Oxford University Press

© Oxford University Press 1985
ISBN 0 19 912056 0

The illustration on p. 129 is by Peter Joyce

Typeset by Avonset, Midsomer Norton, Bath
Printed by Biddles Ltd., Guildford

Contents

Preface	vii
Part I Ends	
1 A language to what purpose?	3
2 The historical ball and chain	22
3 Language learning in the school curriculum	35
Part II Means	
4 The language-experience course	49
5 The specialist course to age 16	76
6 Modern languages in the sixth form	95
7 Language testing	109
8 Classroom aids	127
9 Beyond the classroom: language in use	136
10 To sum up	145
Bibliographical note	150

Preface

'Get out your books, 3Z. Where did we get to last time?' Where indeed! The course book as syllabus, off-the-cuff teaching and inspired ad-libbing: we all know the technique, have seen it in action, have used it (whisper it!) ourselves. But where we got to last time is ultimately determined by where we think we're going to, and if we don't at some stage sit down and ourselves consider that, we shall follow the course book wherever it leads or merely treat each lesson as a holding operation.

This book is about where we've got to, where we may perhaps believe we're going to, who is going where, and how we organize the journey. It may appeal to those just starting out on their teaching careers, whether as student teachers or probationers, and also to those who, having taught for a time, have at last found an hour or two to sit back and contemplate their overall intentions and their daily performance. It may additionally, I hope, lead some Heads of Department to consider the appropriateness of the material they are offering to some of their pupils and its relationship to what they want those pupils to have gained and to be able to do when they finish language learning in school.

I must confess to a pronoun problem when referring to single teachers and pupils. Eventually I have settled on 'she' for the teacher (since modern languages teachers mainly are), 'he' for pupils up to 16+, and (again because they mainly are) 'she' for sixth-formers. By the same reasoning, Heads are 'he'. None of this implies endorsement of the situation!

Similarly, people living outside England in these isles may from time to time have to swallow an 'England' or an 'English'. 'Britain' and 'British' have been used where possible, expressions like 'England and Wales' where ambiguity would otherwise arise, but from time to time only 'England' or 'English' avoids unbearable clumsiness. The same applies at times to the use of 'France' and 'French' instead of 'the Modern Language in question' and 'the country or countries where that language is spoken'. Even the English language has its inadequacies!

My thanks are due to a number of generations of Postgraduate Certificate students at Sheffield University for battering my ideas, shaking my confidence, taking my proposals to pieces, and generally refusing to let my feet leave the ground; and to the pupils whose response to my own developing intentions and style of teaching originally shaped those ideas.

W.R.
July 1983

Part I
Ends

1 A language to what purpose?

For most of this century and longer, the aims, content, method and purpose of modern language teaching have been in dispute. Are we enriching children's minds or giving them a usable career tool? Are they to be taught to read the classics of foreign literature or converse with continental taxi-drivers? Should they commit lists of vocabulary to memory or learn structures? Should they study grammar or practise patterns? Is their classroom time to be spent translating from English or naming objects in the foreign tongue? Can we teach languages in the classroom at all?

The lack of clarity about where we are going, and how, and even why, has led to a series of doubtful medicines readily swallowed as the magic brew that will, after a couple of doses, convert little Kevin into little Jean-Pierre. Thus it was, at the turn of the century and beyond, with phonetics, in the forties with the gramophone record, then the tape recorder, the tape-plus-filmstrip combination — grandly called the audio-visual method —, the language laboratory, modern languages in the primary school. The most recent panaceas are the graded test and perhaps CALL, computer-assisted language learning. None of the past panaceas has lived up to expectations, because the expectations were of magic: few people asked what was possible in the time available and which among the possibilities was desirable. The secondary school child studying a language for five years to 16+ now has typically 380 hours, or 24 waking days, of exposure to that language, experienced in a class of up to 30 pupils; most children drop out of the course long before that modest total of hours is reached. And of course a very great deal of that time is spent on activities other than ingesting and expressing the language.

It is a growing, somewhat uneasy realization of the limited time at our disposal and the acknowledgement that we may have been trying to do too many things in too many ways without thinking through what they involve, that has led to the present situation, some would say of depression and disillusion, some would suggest of growing realism, of *reculer pour mieux sauter*.

Many of the rehearsed arguments about why we learn a foreign language (or indeed, more than one) in our secondary schools look decidedly thin in relation to the time available and the actual classroom experience of our pupils during that time. And many of these paper virtues could be as easily — more easily — acquired through other parts of the school curriculum.

Let us briefly consider some of them. A foreign language, it is said, is a personal way-in to another culture, to a different civilization, to an alternative way of thinking. But how far does the average secondary school pupil penetrate into French civilization? If a breakdown of cultural chauvinism is the main aim, why not teach American civilization, where the pupil already has, more or less, a mastery of the language? Alternatively, or additionally, learning a foreign language may be viewed as representing an extension of general linguistic skills. But if this is the aim, why not substitute a basic course in practical linguistics and teach directly to that aim? (Some schools do in fact teach such a course.) Or are we teaching French and sometimes German to give our children a closer understanding of our nearest neighbours? England's nearest neighbours from a different language community are the Welsh. Historically we are enmeshed with them, geographically they are most accessible. But there is no great movement to teach Welsh in English secondary schools. Could it be we see solidarity, communication, mutual comprehension within the EEC as vitally important? But what then of the non-Common Market languages we teach? Is it mainly that any language learning at school helps you to learn another language later in life when you need it? This last argument sounds suspiciously like the old argument for Latin, that 'it helps you with your French'. The strongest argument for *mastery* of a foreign language, that it enables you to gain a new view of your own culture from the perspective of the foreign one and in doing so enriches *you*, is no argument for the school course: in 24 days you are not going to be able to equip yourself to penetrate so far into the foreign culture that you can see out again on the other side.

The relative weakness of these general educational arguments in relation to what really goes on in the classroom has moved modern language teaching in the last few years into a position of slightly uneasy defensive utilitarianism. The language we teach has got to be useful to justify teaching it at all. The uneasiness stems from the difficulty of predicting what is going to be useful when your constituency of learners is the whole of the population. 'English for Swedish post-office counter clerks' can lead easily to general agreement on a repertoire of useful vocabulary and structure, on the relative importance of each of the skills, on materials and methods appropriate to the age, the social and employment background of the learners, and so on. And the language learned will be immediately used. Our school constituency however is simply 'English-speaking teenagers', and even that may not be entirely true. As a result in the first stage of foreign language learning the utilitarian motivation often now seems to take the form 'What I'm teaching you could be useful on a visit to France'; this later becomes 'This stuff will be useful in the next school exam' and the teacher finally settles for 'This will help you get your O level/CSE/16+'. By this point the examination syllabus, in so far as it actually exists, has become a self-contained, unreferenced thing, the exam a magic talisman. There is an unacknowledged conspiracy between examiner, teacher, and pupil, to limit what is examined, and therefore taught, to arbitrary but known areas that hardly add up to a body of language that can be used for any purpose at all outside the examination itself.

It is really not surprising that pupils who feel that the talisman is out of reach drop out of a long course that seems to move further and further away from personal relevance. The alternative approach, that of teaching a smattering of several languages and civilizations (dignified with the title of European Studies) is really an attempt to keep that initial 'useful on a visit to France' motivation going by extending it through possible visits to Spain, Italy, Germany . . . The lack of success that attends this approach as well comes in part from the growing unreality of 'visits' that do not and are not likely to materialize, and from a growing confusion of unrelated basic phrases from several languages that have never been put to real-life use. This is spurious utilitarianism, a confidence trick that the punter rapidly sees through.

If we are uncertain why we are teaching a foreign language in our secondary schools, can we be clear *which* language we ought to be teaching? So far the author has been careful to use the words 'foreign language' or 'modern languages' to generalize points. In reality the word 'French' could equally well have been used without distorting the facts too much. The statistics speak for themselves:

Examination entries in foreign languages: school leavers in England. Academic year 1981-82. Figures in thousands.

	O level	*CSE*	*A level*
French	157.69	155.80	25.15
German	50.76	33.62	8.90
Spanish	12.87	5.84	2.93
Italian	2.90	0.66	0.74
Russian	1.43	0.24	0.38

16+ entries are included under both O level and CSE.
Source: Examination Boards Survey 1982

For most children their first and only experience of foreign language learning, the language they learn for one, two, at most three years before dropping it, is French. It is fashionable to deplore this concentration on a single language at this stage, but at the same time few steps are taken to destroy the monopoly. This is partly because of the difficulty of defining the aims involved in 'a foreign language for all'. Clearly the argument for keeping languages other than French alive in Britain is a weak one when the end-product for most children is so low a level of language competence anyway. The status quo may in fact make sense in that, if it is felt to be a universally good educational experience to learn to express something, however little, in a tongue other than one's own[1], then a concentration of resources nationally through a single language may be the most effective way of doing this in terms of courses, materials, teacher availability, teacher training, development of methods, teacher interaction, and so on. This sort of language teaching, however, clearly has quite different aims from teaching the *mastery* of a foreign language.

However, even if there is a practical case for the adoption of a single foreign language nationally for 'language-experience' teaching, why French? German is easier in its earliest stages, both in terms of its pronunciation and its large number of homomorphs, and gives a personal stake, however small, in four European countries with very different civilizations and political systems. Spanish is also easier than French in terms of pronunciation and verb use and in common with French offers increased access to and understanding of the more sophisticated, Latin-based vocabulary of our own language. It is also the language of the country where many pupils will have spent their first holidays abroad, though this may be becoming less generally true.

But if one's aim is simply to give the experience of using a foreign tongue to express oneself, the actual language used matters less. French has the very considerable practical advantages of greater availability of teachers, a greater variety and sophistication of published materials, more teaching experience across the ability range, and the easiest accessibility of any truly foreign country.[2] These factors are likely to mean that French will remain the predominant language in terms of short-course language experience for all.

When then should we start French? And which institutions should we teach it in, and how long should courses last? The wonder-drug of the sixties and seventies was Primary French. In the tracks of

Marcelle Kellermann's successful attempts to teach a limited amount of direct-method French to intelligent 10- and 11-year-olds in Leeds[3] a completely different bandwagon rolled in 1963 — French for all from eight onwards, to 14 or even 16 — fuelled by the Nuffield Foundation's grant of a million pounds for materials development.[4] The assumptions of the appropriateness of long-course language learning for all and of the teacher's ability to continue to motivate classroom learning through six or eight years were hardly questioned. The careful monitoring of the scheme by the National Foundation for Educational Research meant that when final judgement of its effectiveness was arrived at[5] the conclusions were difficult to gainsay.[6] The bandwagon ran rapidly off the road and Primary French schemes closed all over the country, not without sighs of relief from many harassed and unconvinced teachers working near the edge of their competence.[7] But the scheme should have taught us some things. Its starting point was the ability of eight-year-olds to acquire the spoken language in an uninhibited, thoughtless way, language geared to their own everyday interests as far as possible rather than to some future 'visit to France'. This is part of a view of foreign language learning as long-term learning for mastery, and in itself presupposes continuing extrinsic motivation throughout the long term. This was not provided: it quickly became clear to children that though it was fun for a time to talk about objects around them and everyday events in a funny code called French, the actual relevance of this to their real life was non-existent. Outside the French lesson no one talked about playing football or eating breakfast in French: these were school rituals unrelated to life in a way that most of the rest of the primary school curriculum was not.[8]

It was not just in terms of relevance to (or enlargement of or explanation of) real life that Primary French was qualitatively different from the rest of the curriculum: there were other elements of Primary French teaching that in terms of the overall philosophy of primary education were always extremely questionable. There was the contrast between the teacher-centred learning of French lessons and discovery methods elsewhere, there was the lack of integration of the foreign language material (and even, often, of its teacher) with work in the rest of the curriculum. There was the fact that most materials for Primary French were developed at a time of maximum belief in behaviourist approaches to foreign-language learning, so that materials and methods concentrated on overlearning structures, rote parroting, the strict limitation of exposure to and production of language, and the avoidance of error (rather than learning from it). All these things contrasted with the greater open-endedness and divergence of primary-school learning in other areas. Perhaps other methodologies might have integrated the foreign language more and made it a more successful part of the educational life of the primary school, though there would still have been the problem of relevance to overcome, as well as the lack of a clear definition of aims. One factor which was never fully appreciated was the need for the personal involvement of the learner. The assumption of a long course from eight means that at the start the amount of personal decision-making about course and content is relatively small. At eight, teacher almost certainly knows best. But by 14, and often long before, the child, now an adolescent, takes a much more active part in his own learning, for good or ill. If he or she decides that French is not for him or her, it won't be, no matter how many French lessons are attended. The assumption that all who start at eight will actively choose to continue to 14 or 16 is clearly idealistic, yet there is no obvious way of determining at eight who the long-term learners may be. We have probably seen the end of the concept of long-term learning from eight for all: indeed with the growth of the graded-test movement the pendulum has swung to the opposite extreme of very short-term learning goals, defined and limited, with a clear achievement at each point and a personal decision whether to attempt the next achievement.

If the early start for all has been shown to be impractical, what of the late start? Questions of *when* a language is learned bring with them the equally important problem of *where*. If languages are banished from the primary school, is the secondary school automatically the best place for language learning? What of sixth forms or sixth-form colleges, what of further education? And if the secondary school *is* the best place, is the five-year drip-feed method most appropriate or are there other ways of organizing learning? The problems of long-term, unflagging motivation that beset the primary start are there too in the 11+ start. Though adolescents are better able to work to long-term goals than young children, the relevance to those goals of what is being done is more sharply questioned. And there are arguments based on motivation, choice, intensity derived from experience of teaching and learning a third language, where a two or three-year course does not appear to be notably less successful than the five-year secondary slog of French.[9] Harry Rée has argued notably for the later start and the more intense (and perhaps thus more realistic) learning experience[10], and schools such as the Archbishop Michael Ramsey School in London have attempted this. Here French is taught for two half-days a week to older (but not unprepared) beginners. Team teaching is used and teaching is largely through the medium of French, taking, for instance, the day's news in French as a starting point. This intensive-bath approach appears to be fairly successful, especially in developing the skill of aural comprehension, but any move towards the adoption of intensive work raises the urgent question of *where*. For the argument can be carried a stage further. If utilitarian considerations are the only ones, then *all* French is French for special purposes. The French Fred needs is different from Mary's because they have different interests and perceptions of life. Does it not in this case make better sense to put all foreign language teaching into Further Education (or more ambitiously, special Language Teaching Centres) where intensive learning with whatever end in view — a job in Brussels, a holiday in Britanny, a girl-friend in Paris — can be organized with a course somewhat more closely tailored to individual motivation and needs? This does not invalidate the argument for some sort of language-learning experience for all in schools, but it does bring into question the appropriateness of the O-level or 16+ course in terms of its utilitarian value and seems to demand justification of the retention of such a course from a general educational standpoint with arguments distinct from those for simple foreign-language learning experience, already catered for by short-course 'French for all'. Any argument in utilitarian terms would involve a careful analysis of the language-content of the course taught and its justification as basic to *any* subsequent special-purpose learning in the language in question. This is far from easy: *und* is self-evidently basic language, *Rheinschiffahrtsgesellschaft* equally self-evidently not; but where *exactly* do you draw the line in between? The classroom course that current examinations at 16+ seem to presuppose would certainly not stand up to this analysis. In general educational terms, on the other hand, any 16+ foreign language course would have to be justified by virtue of its effectiveness in extending general linguistic skills and developing such areas as perception, precision, intelligent guesswork, verbal motor skills, oral self-confidence, personality development through simulation, and so on. The utilitarian arguments for the five-year course seem therefore to revolve around course content, the educational ones around teaching method and learning experience. It is far from clear that the five-year course to 16+ as at present constituted satisfies either utilitarian or general educational criteria.

What ought to be emerging then would appear to be language-learning experience for all, in a discrete short course; long-course learning for some, with the question of *how long* still very open but with a new and much clearer definition of aims in terms of language learned and the educational insights and development to be gained through learning it; special-purpose language-learning available for all, outside compulsory schooling, to which the first two forms of learning can make a contribution in terms of attitudes and insights and, in the case of long-course learning, in terms of useful basic skills.

In point of fact the reality for the foreseeable future is not going to be quite so clear cut. Practical considerations, such as staff in post and a reluctance to leave all long-course or specialist foreign language learning in the non-compulsory area of education (what if no one chooses to learn languages?) are going to mean in many schools a two-year course of language-learning experience for all, followed by a specialist, quasi-optional course or courses of specialism to 16+. In some schools the general course will be three years, the subsequent specialist course only two. There is bound to be, however, with post-16 rationalization, a greater variety of continuation courses at sixth-form level, taught in fewer places, and with fewer pupils opting for the increasingly unpopular traditional A-level prose and literature course.

Consequential changes in the way we teach are necessary and are already occurring. New and different aims in the language-experience courses mean new and wider-ranging methods. The 13+ or 14+ beginners are in many respects *faux débutants* and need a different teaching style and different materials. Third language teachers will even more than in the past find themselves teaching older students, with the more adult approach and relationships with pupils that this involves.

The foreign-language teacher will also find herself — is finding herself — teaching the same all-embracing ability range of children in the early secondary years as her colleagues in other subjects, and teaching therefore, like her colleagues, a course whose core consists of elements that can be absorbed by a broad spectrum of abilities. Further up the school, for the pre-16+ years, she will find herself teaching a differently organized course with different aims, at a different pace, with more specialized and more intensive work to adolescents with different motivations. In areas such as Leeds with 13+ transfer we may in fact be talking here of two quite different teachers in different institutions, but in most areas both types of teaching will be a necessary part of each day's work for most teachers. And a substantial proportion of them will find themselves additionally teaching intensive courses in their first or second foreign language to older learners with a more specific, practical aim in view. All this means that 'foreign language teaching' is no longer a single occupation, but two or even three distinct, if overlapping, skilled jobs. Different tools and different methods are needed for each.[11]

Much of the discussion above implies that whatever the age and type of foreign language learning, it will take place in some institution: primary school, comprehensive, sixth-form college, Further Education college, Language Teaching Centre ... But institutional walls are coming down both to let the pupil out and to let the country whose language is being learnt in. It is becoming easier to prove to the pupil that it is reality that is being dealt with and not just a code invented by the languages teacher for her own convenience and regular salary cheque. Visits abroad are not new but are becoming more purposeful and more effectively designed to involve the pupil in the life of the foreign country rather than simply allowing him or her to behave as a passive observer. Audio recordings have been freed from the tyranny of the BBC's timetable and have become portable, so that material on cassette can be listened to anywhere and at any time. Video recordings on more compact machines are beginning to do the same for television programmes and films. Schools are becoming more aware of the foreign language assistant as a living resource at all levels in the school rather than simply as a sixth-form supplement. Foreign radio, still photographs and slides, real current magazines, newspapers, records, foreign visitors, *correspondance sonore*, term exchanges, French-speaking residential courses[12] — all these windows on to the reality of the foreign country, where the language really has to be used as a tool of genuine communication and understanding rather than as part of a teacher-defined game, are becoming more and more common as schools realize that the only lasting motivation on their pupils' part is the knowledge that the skills they have learnt can be used to some personal profit, and that further progress would mean even greater profit. So more and more in the most successful language teaching the country is brought into the classroom and the classroom taken into the country.

If these then are our language-course alternatives, what exactly should be our language targets? What skills should we aim for on these various types of language course? Let us first consider the short course for all, the language-experience course.

What we teach depends on why we are teaching it. One approach to the language-experience course is to teach a 'survival kit'. These are based on the teacher's intuition (or the course writer's) of what her pupils are likely to use at the most basic level on a visit to the country. This may or may not be accurate: what one really needs to survive is not always classroom taught, even on survival-kit courses. A recent visit to rural Turkey by the author, who speaks no Turkish, brought this vividly home. The trip was largely self-catering. Nouns proved most vital: basic foodstuffs, drinks, and facilities; numbers; directions; the ability to transfer written information (on labels, for instance) into the spoken form; question words like *where is?, how much?;* politeness words like *thank you very much, please, excuse me, great!* (quite vital, these). Complicated comprehension ability is not necessary, since interlocutors, realizing they are dealing with a linguistic baby, themselves lapse into a pidgin form of their language with precisely pronounced nouns, few verbs, large gestures. For sheer survival not much else is required. A survival kit of this kind could be covered in a term with the slowest class and in theory offered in French, German, and Spanish in a year. Aside from any question of the educational value of three survival kits, would their contents stick? These snowflakes of language will only remain and accrete if the pupil's interest continues, which in turn depends on what is learnt being put to use. Language defined in this narrowly utilitarian way is only of value if it *is* of genuine utility. An actual visit to the country at the end of the course, for which the course prepares, can provide this.[13] A graded test can go some way towards doing this too, though here as with all examinations the certificate rather than the skill can easily come to take precedence. The end-product of the course is all too often seen by the pupil as the embossed card pinned to the bedroom wall rather than the skill this is meant to denote. Ultimately language will only stick if it is embedded in a real context or an intellectual construct. *Apfelsinen* (N. German = oranges) will be learnt if it was directly associated with buying luscious oranges under that funny Roland statue in the crowded and picturesque market-place in Bremen, or if it takes its place in some intellectual framework: *Apfelsine* = apple of China . . . the golden apples of the Hesperides . . . pomodoro . . . pomegranate. . . It is far less likely to be a permanent acquisition if it is simply a code-word for orange.

So if we settle, as some schools do, for a survival kit or kits as our language experience, then some genuine experience of language use as the end-product seems necessary. Immediately we move beyond this, and especially when we move beyond the basic language-experience course to one leading to some sort of competence at 16+, questions arise of which specific skills to teach and with what relative emphasis.

One of the 'discoveries' of the sixties was that language learning can be separated into four skills: aural and visual comprehension, oral and written production. This *aperçu,* though fairly obvious, none the less concentrated teachers' (and course writers') minds on the best way of developing each individual skill, and also raised more forcibly the question of their relative values.[14] In a utilitarian view of language learning it was clearly the two spoken word skills that were paramount and it is these that now, at any rate in theory, dominate the early years of language learning in a language-experience course and play a large part at the start of long-course learning as well. For many children a measure of competence in the spoken word might seem to be an appropriate language target at stages beyond the mere survival kit. Usually an informal, though not colloquial, register is taught, with language based on a limited number of situations and areas, and functions associated with those situations and areas. This sort of work is typical of first-stage graded syllabuses, the situations usually revolving around tourist experiences, visiting a foreign home, and descriptions of self.[15] Interestingly the teacher or course designer is here making value judgements about what is or should be important, useful, and interesting to the learner, just as much as with older long-term examination syllabuses: the feedback to both teacher and learner, in terms of examination success or failure and stay-on for the next stage, is however more immediate.

Within the area of the spoken word the question of the relative importance of comprehension and production arises. At a stage slightly beyond the pidgin of the survival kit, production might seem to be easier for the learner than comprehension. The onus of making sense of the non-native's mixture of error and correctness lies on the much better equipped native listener. Comprehension for the learner is much more difficult. Inexperienced as he is, when faced with a native he none the less has to disentangle not just word from word but accent, unknown vocabulary and structure, speed, ellipsis, colloquialism, speech idiosyncrasy or even defect in the native speaker. However, for once the classroom does not impose quite such harsh limitations as it usually does, in that with a class of thirty or so pupils, given a tape recorder or the foreign assistant, it is much easier to provide extended experience of listening comprehension (and produce evidence of progress that helps keep motivation high) than of oral production. At this stage one target might well be polyglot conversation, in which each interlocutor speaks his own language but understands the other. This form of conversation, that arises when each speaker has more passive than active knowledge of the other's language, is rather common in practice. Frowned on by language purists, it none the less can produce surprisingly sophisticated exchanges among speakers who can express themselves in the foreign language only slowly and with hesitation.

A more ambitious target for a basic course is a degree of aural/oral competence plus reading comprehension. This is the aim of most CSE courses. The purely aural/oral start with no printed-word back-up at all, popular in the early days of the so-called audio-visual method of the sixties, died out as it became clear that for many learners the printed word was a vital prop to organized and precise learning. For such learners the printed word even at the earliest stage meant greater facility in acquiring the spoken word, giving it an additional context, chaining it more securely to homomorphs in English, above all helping to give a feeling of confidence in learning. In non-phonetic languages like French (and especially English, of course) there is a price to pay in the non-concordance of printed and spoken word and in the more difficult morphology of the printed language.[16] Equally, though, the multiplicity of printed-word markers makes reading (as opposed to written production) that much easier. A sentence such as *C'est les oiseaux bleus qui chantent* has four markers for plurality in the written language to combat the distracting singular *c'est*. There is only one such marker (the [e] of *les*) in spoken French. In terms of realism and utility the reading of some items — notices, labels — is necessary even at the very earliest stage. At a later stage the spoken language benefits from reinforcement by, transfer from, and interaction with, the written word. Furthermore reading, silent reading that is, is perhaps the easiest area in which to develop true pupil autonomy in the classroom (aural comprehension comes next). Because it is easy to organize efficiently in the classroom it gives a considerable chance of fairly early success, of the feeling in the learner that he is getting somewhere and doing something for himself. Comprehension, whether of the printed or the spoken word, is the area where the learner can most easily be weaned from attention to medium to attention to message.

In courses of this kind the role of grammar, the type of grammar, the amount of grammar have all become problematic. For a time grammar became a dirty word for many language teachers. Teachers of earlier generations had made grammar the centre of language learning, partly because in their classroom situation and with the materials and methods available it was one of the very few aspects of the foreign language easily teachable. Most pupils brought up in this way became adults without an ability to communicate in the foreign language and often with a great deal of resentment against the language teaching they had experienced. With the rise of the audio-visual 'method' in the fifties and sixties some teachers (though perhaps fewer than might have been thought at the time) jettisoned grammar in favour of rote learning of phrase or structure. That this total rejection of grammar was less than whole-hearted and relatively short-lived was certainly because classroom teachers recognized that for any real mastery and confident production of the foreign language grammatical insight is useful for most learners and vital for many.

The *necessary* grammar, though, is somewhat different from the grammar of the grammar-centred method. To start with it is insightful: from the learner's point of view it is, or should be, 'descriptive of what we're doing' rather than 'prescriptive of what we should do'. The generative rules that the learner eventually establishes to decode and produce language are much subtler and at a deeper level than the grammar rules of the textbook; but the latter are an explanatory starting point in the process of laying down the former, and a monitor of correctness *after* production. The explanatory grammar that a pupil learns forms a scaffolding to which further language items may be attached as they are learnt. Their placing on this framework helps their retention. But clearly the grammar framework needs to be appropriate to the type of learning intended. In the past much grammar was included in modern language teaching simply because it paralleled Latin grammar or because it could be enunciated simply or elegantly. The rules for agreement of the past participle with the preceding direct object in French are a good example of the latter. This is a self-contained set of rules, not too difficult to master, easily applied to endless simple written exercises. It therefore took (indeed, often still takes!) a prominent part in the teaching of the perfect tense. In fact, if the aim is accurate expression in the spoken language, time spent on the preceding direct object agreement is virtually wasted, since almost no verbs show it in their spoken form. If understanding the language, either spoken or written, is the aim, then again the time is wasted since as a marker the preceding direct object agreement, where perceivable, is almost invariably redundant. It is only in the production of written French that any sort of case may be made out, and even here in terms of communication its importance is trivial in comparison with, say, correct word order of pronoun objects and negatives in the compound tenses.

But the grammar framework needs to be appropriate not only to the *type* of learning intended, but also to the stage reached. Many teachers find it difficult to accept that all grammar 'rules' are ultimately over-generalizations, part-truths, limited maps to help one find one's way through the bit of wood one is currently traversing. To 'know' that all prepositions in German are followed by dative *-em* or *-er* endings is a helpful rule when all the prepositions so far met have taken the dative. It is no help at all to be told by a teacher with a misplaced sense of probity that there are other prepositions that take the accusative, some that take the accusative or the dative in differing circumstances, others that take the genitive, some that take the genitive or the dative according to register or type of object and one at least (the *für* in *was für*) that apparently takes no case at all![17]

If the grammar taught needs to be appropriate to aim and to stage reached, it also needs to be genuinely explanatory. Some basic technical terms need to be taught where they form a useful shorthand, but labels for their own sake, a status-promoting jargon that itself has to be laboriously learned — this is counter-productive. One of the most depressing lessons the author ever observed was taught by a highly-gifted linguist entirely in French, and consisted solely of grammar explanation with the whole panoply of technical terms deployed, this followed by a detailed question-and-answer session in which pupils, with some help from a blackboard glossary, were expected to regurgitate, still in French, these grammar rules. These were intelligent children, and some French was learned during the lesson, but of a kind that was of no practical use at all. The grammar point could have been simply elicited or explained in English in five or ten minutes towards the end of the lesson and the rest of the time taken in practice and use, embodying the grammar point in real French applied in a likely situation or situations. The teacher prided herself on a good lesson in which not a word of English had been spoken!

It seems clear that the long-term learner will need an explanatory framework of grammar, whether his course materials are explicitly organized to help him develop this progressively or not. If the three criteria mentioned above of appropriateness to aim and stage and genuine illumination are kept in mind, a very simple grammar framework can usually be helpful to the short-term learner as well.

This leaves us with the most criticized aspect of modern language teaching: the classroom language teacher's devotion to the fourth skill, the written word. Almost all language teachers would agree, some reluctantly it is true, that ability to use the written word for all except a tiny minority of learners is a goal useless in its own right.[18] And yet almost all language teachers continue to use the written word, at least as a teaching aid. It is relatively productive, highly examinable, clearly has reinforcement value and (not by any means the least consideration) represents a change of activity that will help keep 3Z quiet. It is also almost certainly the aspect of language work that is easiest to teach and administer in a large class. The all too obvious danger is that its various virtues subvert its use as a teaching aid and lead the tired, harassed, overworked or (whisper it, such there be) linguistically incompetent teacher to make it central to her teaching and to make some competence in the production of written French or German her major teaching aim. Pupils, of course, rapidly sense when a teacher has done this, and since for many, perhaps most of them, conformity to the standards of authority is seen as the key to a quiet and (in its own terms) successful life, they will quite readily acquiesce. In any case, from a learner's point of view this is an easier, less demanding, less exposed skill to acquire than the others. *Post hoc* rationalizations by written-word teachers are many and easy: 'The children prefer it. It's good intellectual discipline. It's real learning. You can monitor their progress properly. It's the best possible preparation for their examination.'

The last point has undoubtedly some truth in it. If examination boards continue to test mainly written skills[19] they can hardly expect teachers to prepare for these examinations by teaching spoken skills. Even CSE boards pay only lip-service to spoken production as far as the Mode 1 papers (*papers* — note the word!) of most boards are concerned. And although the O-level boards have been introducing more aural comprehension tests, many of these are more than a little suspect. An intelligent French speaker can, for instance, correctly answer a large part of some sections of the Joint Matriculation Board's O-level 'aural' comprehension paper without listening to the tape provided for aural comprehension *at all*, merely by intelligently putting together clues from the setting and the questions and multiple-choice answers given in the accompanying printed test paper.[20] Testing of oral production at O and A level continues to be a peripheral and hit-and-miss affair. With our present ill-defined, old-fashioned public examinations, inappropriate in the skills they test, teachers can hardly be blamed for some concentration on written work in the run-up to the examination. How this may be more productive and useful is discussed in Chapter 5.

But arguments for the amount of written work still undertaken in many schools in classes remote from external examinations or in non-examination classes are much more defensive and questionable. They centre mainly round the question 'How do I get through a double period without it?' and really form a special case of the general argument for variety of approach and individualized work. At any level of teaching written work can be a haven of comparative quiet for the less competent teacher: the desire to extend the peace (or armistice) is great and too often succumbed to. It rarely produces inspiring work or residual learning of any real value for most pupils.

Finally among skill targets, let us consider translation. Translation into the foreign language as an examining device is slowly dying at 16+, partly because the received wisdom from linguists, teacher trainers and course compilers has been against it as a skill (as opposed to a technique of testing) at this level for a generation. It has to be recognized that any examination technique feeds back into its preparatory course and that if it is not a desirable skill to be taught it should not be included as a test. It is difficult in any case to justify the croquet course of grammar hoops represented by the average O-level prose either as a test or as a skill in its own right. But is there perhaps something of value being lost as the prose slowly disappears from view?

Though, at the level that concerns us here, most translation into the foreign language has been merely a form of grammar reinforcement exercise, with the desired end-product firmly in the prose compiler's mind as she produced forms of English that would inevitably lead to a single, correct foreign language version, at A level (theoretically and sometimes also in practice) and at university level prose translation is an open-ended exercise that demands a high sensitivity to both the languages involved and a creative search for correspondences between them. There is an equivalent exercise to this at the level of 16+ and below, which is different from the prose translation of a doctored piece of English aiming to test mastery of various points of French grammar. This consists of an exercise in 'interpreting' at a low level in which the pupil is asked to convey in the foreign language a number of pieces of information given to him in English, or to put a series of questions in the foreign language that will elicit desired information, again given him in English. This corresponds closely to the kind of language interpreting inevitably undertaken by anyone with any knowledge of a foreign language who is accompanied in the country by a non-speaker of that language — 'Ask him for a boiled egg', 'See if they've got any paper hankies', 'Find out when the next steamer up the Bosphorus goes'. What goes on next in real life is a very simple version of the 'creative search for correspondence' of the university prose translation of a page of Dickins. The word for paper handkerchief may be invented or paraphrased and used in whatever request format is most comfortable to the speaker, with a final foreign language version some distance from the original English of his companion. This form of 'translation' has a clear utilitarian value at the level we are dealing with and it is by no means impossible to establish it in an oral form in the classroom. Its written equivalent has some practical value, too, in eliciting information in writing ('Drop them a line and find out if they've a double room for the 27th, then.')

What however of translation into English from the foreign language? The easily graded multiple-choice objective test has eclipsed translation as a form of testing. Its simplicity of administration, if not of devising, has made the multiple-choice test very readily accepted. Perhaps too readily, since there are some quite serious doubts as to what it tests, how effective it is, and what its effects are on the pupil's view of foreign language learning. Within most teaching strategies the formal translation of a passage of printed French into polished written English has become rare, though informal translation as a comprehension check is still widely used, even where use of the foreign language is maximized, as a rapid, precise, and unambiguous feedback to the teacher that the meaning of a word or phrase has been understood. One of the lessons learned the hard way by many teachers from the audio-visual courses of the sixties was that pupils who learn sound sequences with no idea or an imprecise idea of their meaning make no progress and build up a deep and lasting resentment against the method or indeed against the whole subject. English-to-check has been rediscovered as an important tool leaving both pupils and teacher more confident in what has been taught. Translation of heard French into spoken English, though much less used, has something to commend it if it is seen as the reverse process to interpreting into the foreign language. It is an unconstrained and realistic exercise, with the gist of the heard foreign language, including all important points, to be conveyed orally in the pupil's own language. Again, the precise nature of the feedback to both teacher and learner helps build confidence.

Whatever the language teacher sees as her proper teaching aim in relation to a particular child or group of children, she is going to be constrained by the sanctions applied externally, the examination syllabus she is working with. Even CSE Mode 3 and graded tests are, for the ordinary teacher arriving newly in a school, often just as externally pre-ordained as O level or CSE Mode 1. But if part of her purpose must in most schools be to aim her pupils at a specific, externally determined target, it is still possible, as we shall see, for the aware teacher to include this target within her language-teaching objectives without making it her only, or her qualitatively most important, goal.

Which language, when and where, even to a large extent why, may be out of the hands of the individual teacher in terms of her everyday teaching. The skills she promotes and the balance of skills are more under her control, the methods she uses even more so. But even methods, considered in detail in Part II, are subject to constraint through imposed attitudes and values. These are to a considerable extent historically determined, and we shall be weighing this historical ball and chain in the next chapter.

Footnotes

[1] And this seems the strongest educational argument for some experience of language learning as part of a universal core curriculum: the realization that word and object are not one and the same thing, that there are other ways of expressing the world than the one so far learned.

[2] Not just for the south-east. Schools in Rotherham and Sheffield known to the author organize day-trips by bus to Calais. A long day, but the fact that you can demonstrably get there and back in a day on a bus does wonders for the perceived reality of France in South Yorkshire.

[3] See Kellermann M. *Two experiments on language teaching in primary schools* Nuffield Foundation 1964.

[4] The UK Primary scheme was only one of several around the world at this time, with the Council of Europe amongst others actively promoting a foreign language for all from around ten, and calling for experiments with earlier starting ages.

[5] Burstall C. *et al. Primary French in the Balance* 1974 NFER.

[6] Though some attempts were made. The most interesting are: Bennett S. N. 'Weighing the evidence' 1945 *BJEP* 45; Gamble C. J. and Smalley A. 'Primary French in the Balance: Were the scales accurate?' *Modern Languages* VI, 2 1975; Buckby M. 'Is Primary French really in the Balance?' *Audio-Visual Language Journal* 14 1976; Stern H. H. 'Optional age: Myth or Reality?' *Canadian Modern Language Review* 32, 3 1976.

[7] Primary French in other countries met a similar lack of success at about the same time.

[8] These same points are equally valid in secondary courses that claim teenage relevance in a context of entirely classroom-bound learning. Adolescents will suspend disbelief for a time, given interesting enough materials

or a teacher they like sufficiently, but to ask for this for eight years or even for five is extremely unrealistic.

⁹ There is Canadian research evidence that suggests that concentrated effort in shorter courses is more effective than a small daily dose of language work over a longer period. See Stern H. H. 'The Ottawa-Carleton French project' *Canadian Modern Languages Review* 33, 2, 216–32 (1976), and Stern H. H. *et al. Three Approaches to teaching French* Toronto, Ontario Ministry of Education 1976.

¹⁰ In, for example, the Times Educational Supplement of 11.1.80: 'Why Foreign Languages don't belong in any core curriculum'.

¹¹ Graded objectives and tests, as at present conceived, fit most happily into the first kind of learning, in that they tend to limit the language specified to allow a high percentage of pupils to master the material. They are convergent rather than divergent. They make sense for a limited language-experience course across the ability range: they may fit less happily with the more open-ended aims of long-term learning.

¹² None of these is especially novel: the author was organizing term exchanges back in the early sixties. It is the global attitude to them as central and essential rather than desirable extras that has changed.

¹³ Few courses actually do this. An honourable, pioneering exception back in 1970 was the Somerset European Studies syllabus.

¹⁴ It also tended to obscure the interrelated nature of the skills.

¹⁵ The Sheffield syllabus, for instance, specifies as first level topic areas: Café, Restaurant, Meals, Shopping, Town, and House, together with the eliciting and giving of information.

¹⁶ Do you remember — the author does — the sheer horror as a beginner in discovering that [kɛskɔsɛ] was spelled *qu'est-ce que c'est?*

¹⁷ J. A. Comenius put it succinctly, as so often, back in the seventeenth century: 'The teacher should teach not as much as he himself can teach, but as much as the learner can grasp.'

¹⁸ How much actual writing in your first foreign language do *you* do in the course of a year, school work aside? A few letters, and then?

¹⁹ The section on CSE syllabuses and papers in C. Vaughan James and Sonia Rouve's *Survey of Curricula and Performance in Modern Languages* CILT 1973 showed just how heavily reliant testing was, even at this level, on comprehension of the *written* word. Moys A. *et al. Modern Languages Examination at 16 plus* CILT 1980 shows there has been only very limited progress in this respect over nearly a decade.

²⁰ The author's Postgraduate Certificate students of French regularly guess between 80% and 100% correctly on this section of the paper without hearing the aural comprehension test at all.

2 The historical ball and chain

It is easy, and rather dangerous, to view language-teaching methodology, and indeed other aspects of education also, as a continuous upward progress through history. This view recognizes that there have been occasional setbacks and difficulties, but generally sees an upward path illuminated by growing scientific insight and culminating in today's practice, not yet perfect but moving towards perfection. Involved in this attitude is the occasional not too precise glance at assumptions, approaches, methods, courses, syllabuses, examinations of previous times followed by pious astonishment that their perpetrators could be so obtuse, out-of-touch, ill-informed, or downright foolish. But in fact a closer reading of older books on language teaching may well surprise: you may be struck by how much there is, once you have allowed for those often trivial matters and attitudes which are specific to the age, that coincides with modern ideas. Read Jespersen or Comenius and you find yourself constantly saying 'But I thought that was a new idea.' And these two have much in common with each other, over 250 years, as well as with modern ideas.

Methodologies are as much a product of their times as educational systems, and equally rooted in the ideas of their time. Ideas, too, have a habit of coming into and going out of fashion. What is taught and how it is taught is a product of these ideas, as well as of the conditions in which it is to be taught. It is society that determines the content of education, in the light of the dominant philosophy and (more recently) scientific concept. Many, perhaps most, new approaches are rediscoveries of old methods neglected and left in the shade, now re-illuminated by the light of social need. Language teaching, like all other teaching, reflects the temper of the times.

In medieval Europe the foreign language taught was Latin: before the thirteenth century no languages other than Latin and Greek were formally taught. Latin, though, was not just a *lingua franca*; it was the key to the world of scholarship and, from the Renaissance on, to the classical treasure-house of learning. There was a model for this medieval position of Latin in the role of Greek in ancient Rome itself. Then, ironically, Latin was the relatively despised vernacular and Greek the key to all learning, literature, philosophy. The cultivated Roman, like the medieval scholar, had to be bilingual.

The rise of the vernaculars and their diffusion through the new technology of printing meant a gradual separation of functions: Latin was still the key to literature and thought, the essential tool for any sort of education, but more and more through the fifteenth, sixteenth, and seventeenth centuries the vernaculars took over its social role as a language of everyday communication. Gradually Latin ceased to be taught as, say, English is taught in India and became a thing apart from society in general. So methods were adapted to roles. Modern languages where taught were taught by oral methods for communicative purposes, Latin (and Greek) mainly by book methods for literary and philosophical use.

The most famous language teacher and methodologist of this time was the Moravian J. A. Comenius (1592–1670) and it is significant that his concern was initially with the teaching of Latin and his works were written in Latin. An ecclesiastic as well as a teacher, which was not unusual for his time, Comenius was unusual for the time in that he had had some training as a teacher and his writings are derived from his own experience. His works stress the importance of the senses, their role in combination with the word in understanding and retention, and the importance of physical activity in the classroom. He is best known for his use of pictures in language teaching, but in fact he saw them only as a substitute for the real thing. His *Orbis sensualium pictus* (1654) is often cited as a forerunner of the audio-visual method: it is in fact a sequence of numbered picture vocabularies (in Latin plus three vernaculars, German, Hungarian, and Czech). It may equally be seen as the forerunner of the disposable workbook (Comenius wanted the pupils to colour in the illustrations) at a time when textbooks of any kind were still scarce in the classroom, and for all the pupils in a class to have the same textbook was a rarity.

Much in Comenius is quite surprisingly modern:

'The exemplar should always come first, the precept should always follow, and imitation should always be insisted on.'[1]

'The short before the long, the simple before the complex, the general before the particular, the nearer before the more remote, the regular before the irregular.'[2]

Comenius in his early works sees language in use as the starting point, reality as all-important, grammar as secondary and the language classroom as a place where the senses rather than the mind come first. 'The Comenian classroom was one in which both teacher and pupils were in constant activity.'[3] And yet by the end of his life Comenius had himself done a *volte face*, was renouncing his earlier methods and was proposing the derivation of language by the learner from a pre-learned set of rules of grammar. What had happened? Was this simply a step towards reaction in an old man?

What had in fact happened was the dawn of the Age of Reason. Comenius stands at a watershed, at the end of the dominance of the Renaissance view of life, of education, and especially of the Renaissance view of the role of Latin.[4] The Renaissance man was a doer, the seventeenth- and eighteenth-century man was a thinker. Language for the Cartesian man of reason was governed by the same logic that governed all things: the basic rules of one language were the same as those of all languages. They were embedded in its grammar and the art of translation was a central one, involving the manipulation of universals. Surface appearances might be different, underlying laws were essentially the same.[5] The Grammar-Translation method was born as a new, insightful way of approaching language learning that was exactly in tune with the times, with their emphasis on the primacy of reason, law, logic. It superseded the older more pragmatic oral approaches because its apparent precision and universality gave it a prestige in the eyes of an age that valued these qualities highly. Interestingly, it first made its way in the teaching of modern languages, with the classics (where it eventually became most firmly entrenched) adopting its precepts and methods whole-heartedly only at the start of the nineteenth century. In Britain the pre-eminence it retained through the nineteenth century was related to the ethos of an education system geared to the development of logical thinking and to teaching an élite of cultivated minds.

Modern foreign languages, as well as the classics, as taught in the schools of the nineteenth century, could hardly be justified in utilitarian terms for empire-builders or industrialists in what was clearly the most important country in the world: in such terms they were merely for the specialist. But as part of the development of the mind, a continuation of the eighteenth century's placing of logic, scientific logic, in the central position, there was much sense in language learning and language manipulation through a set of grammar rules that brought logic and as far as possible universal applicability to the fore. And methods were tailored to these ends. If modern languages were seen as inferior to classical ones in these terms it was not only because the classics still gave access to the great storehouse of literary and philosophical models, but also because the classical languages, being dead, could not be interfered with by inconsiderate foreigners who actually spoke them, altered them, and often refused to follow the rules of the grammar book. They were more easily treated as a self-contained system.

It was the rise of universal education (and especially, in Britain, the growth of the maintained grammar schools as a result of the 1902 Act) that began the swing of the pendulum in the twentieth century back towards a more pragmatic, more communicative approach. There were movements already in this direction on the continent, fuelled by the newly developed 'science' of phonetics and its apologist Henry Sweet, and by popularizers such as Viëtor, whose pamphlet 'Die Sprachunterricht muß umkehren' (1882) became the bible of the evangelists of the New or Direct (or a dozen other similar attributives) Method.

Seen on this sort of time-scale the various movements and methods of the twentieth century come together as a single reaction, more in tune with the pragmatism and the educational democracy of the times, turning away from reason, the mind, law, and logic as the highest goods. Moreover, they are moving not so much forward as round to the Renaissance position, so that Comenius's earlier writings are rediscovered as startlingly consonant with the position that has now been reached.[6] In these terms the twentieth-century experience can be seen not so much as a group of radicals battling with reactionaries, as the rediscoverers of Renaissance man fighting the inheritors of the age of Reason.

Let us now look at our twentieth-century battles in more detail, for it is only in this way that we can see why one textbook is so heavily weighted towards structure drills, why another course has no textbook at all, why this examination is heavy on multiple-choice tests, why that one still insists on the virtue of prose translation. And we may perhaps see that we are not on a broad uphill road to better and better methodology and more and more efficient teaching, but that methods and materials are necessarily a reflection of aims and purposes which in turn lie in the changing structure and values of the society around us.

The label that has survived today from the nineteenth century is the Direct Method. In content it seems to go back to J. S. Blackie, a Scottish classics teacher who in the 1850s was advocating (one might say re-advocating) the avoidance of the mother tongue, the direct association of word with object, and the relegation of grammar to a subordinate position.[7] The new method attempted to legitimate itself by reference to the way a child learns its first language[8], but it was phonetics which appeared to give both a scientific respectability and also a way round the doubtful and difficult orthography of the printed word and the attendant stress on reading and writing. Above all it seemed to provide easy classroom access to communication in society rather than to literature in the study.

At first the reform methods made slow progress. From the central place that language learning had had in the medieval and Renaissance curricula, it had by the nineteenth century been pushed to the periphery, partly because its aims had remained unchanged from those of the eighteenth century, as had its methods, largely Grammar-Translation. Thus nothing obviously relevant was being taught, and the 'mental discipline' aspect of the work, central to the approach and method originally, was felt to be far better catered for by classics and mathematics. Those modern language teachers who were concerned to transform their discipline in the direction of language for communication came together for the first time in a national conference in 1890 and two years later formed the Modern Languages Association. This was something of a turning-point for the new methods in Britain. The teachers were inspired by the German debate surrounding Viëtor's pamphlet (Viëtor himself addressed the 1890 conference) and passed resolutions supporting oral work, direct method, and the use of phonetics.

The turn of the century also produced notable and influential publications. Sweet's *The Practical Study of Languages* (1899) is particularly concerned to deny the 'universal rule' ideas of Cartesian thought that, however debased, underlay the Grammar-Translation methods of his time. Exposure to the language is the banner he fights under, with phonetics as his big guns. The language comes first: 'listen before you imitate', phonetics allows precise recording of what is heard, and what *is* heard will be arbitrary, not the product of pre-learned rules. The work is a clear pointer to the behaviourist approaches of the audio-lingual school, but also, in its insistence on a broad exposure to language, a pointer, too, to some of the criticisms made of them.

However, the man whose name is most closely associated with the Direct Method is Otto Jespersen, Professor of English at the University of Copenhagen, whose book *Sprogundervisning* (translated into English in 1904 as *How to Teach a Foreign Language*) had tremendous success. The *Academy* magazine wrote of a later edition of it 'The Reform method of teaching has prevailed and to no one is more honour due for the victory than the distinguished Danish linguist and teacher, Dr Otto Jespersen.' And in fact its successes included the adoption of this method as the sole one to be used in schools by France, Belgium, and Germany. This book is an easily read, common-sense, practical work that assumes communication as an end and suggests a range of means, most of which would be acceptable to the modern comprehensive school teacher with the same end in view (the notable exception is the stress on phonetics). Like Comenius's work, Jespersen's book seems surprisingly modern only because similar aims tend to produce similar methods. He advocates natural, useful language material, careful listening, direct association of word with object or idea, grammar derived from language known, and the foreign language as the principal if not only means of communication in the classroom.

The Direct Method in fact failed in Britain (though not in Germany) for a number of reasons. Circular 797 of 1912 of the Board of Education ('Modern Languages') reporting on it, says categorically 'the staff is unequal to the task'. But it is also clear that the task was misunderstood. Phonetic script (the technological panacea of the time) was introduced by many schools, but not the aim of communicative ability, and thus only some of the precepts and methods of the reformers were adopted and mixed with the traditional approach. There was some excuse for this, since the schools were of necessity working towards traditional examinations. It is probably true to say that the Direct Method did not fail in England: it was never properly tried. And if there was in the first years of the century a growing public concern to improve language teaching for communication, the trauma of the First World War changed this almost completely.

The chauvinism produced by the war in a generation of schoolchildren and their teachers for perhaps a dozen years from 1914 enabled those forces to triumph that were concerned to maintain language teaching in the literary/mental discipline mode. These were above all the universities, both in the context of their own courses and the implied prerequisites for them, and in their control of the new School Certificate and Higher School Certificate examinations from 1917 onwards. The teaching force, too, was weakened by the wholesale slaughter of the war years, but even more, public opinion became inward-looking, anti-European and especially anti-German. Language learning in the schools reflected this and language as abstract logic gained in respectability.

However, the movement towards language for communication

was still there, though battered. In Harold Palmer it had a new guru. His *Scientific Study and Teaching of Languages* (1917) and later works such as *The Principles of Language Study* (1921) and *This Language-learning Business* (with H. V. Redman, 1932) discarded pure Direct Method, pointing out its fallacies, and liberated the teacher from her most difficult (and perhaps impossible) task, the conveyance of meaning entirely in the foreign language. At the same time Palmer's approach allowed and encouraged her in strategies for maximizing teaching efficiency still with communication as her goal.

Palmer saw the need to fit the language course to the aims of the actual students rather than some abstract goal: 'We cannot design a language course until we know something about the students for whom the course is intended, for a programme of study depends on the aim or aims of the students. All we can say in advance is that we must endeavour to utilize the most appropriate means to attain the desired end.'[9] Palmer was suspicious of panaceas, of uncritical acceptance of one right way in anything; none the less, he believed in the need for exposure to the language, and advocated the pupils' complete immersion in the foreign language for a period before being allowed to use it. He himself exposed his pupils to the foreign language for three months before allowing them to use it.[10] To Palmer we also owe the first large-scale and systematic working-out and use of the pattern drill. Palmer was the first person to point out the difference between intensive and extensive reading and to draw lessons from this for the language classroom including the use of silent reading. He was consciously eclectic: method was 'the multiple line of approach'.[11] But he differentiated between 'studial' approaches to language learning and unconscious assimilation, realizing that what coursebook and teacher intend is different from what each individual pupil learns. In this he goes a long way towards the important distinction made by Stephen Krashen[12] between the imposed process of Learning and the self-organized, subconscious process of Acquisition. None the less, overall Palmer relies heavily on habit-forming drills designed to ensure 'automatism'. He is aware of the potential monotony of this, but not much attention is paid to ways of motivating the student to use, actively and realistically, the language he has acquired. Palmer's six basic principles were: **1** ears before eyes; **2** reception before reproduction; **3** oral repetition before reading (he means reading aloud); **4** immediate memory before prolonged memory (proficiency in the 'just-heard' is most important); **5** chorus work before individualized work; **6** drill work before free work. There are certainly echoes of Comenius here!

Palmer's ideas were generally practical and represented a considerable step in the direction of communication. Movement in this direction was also helped by the fact that as the effects of the war became less immediate, public opinion gradually became more outward-looking. And now there were more language graduates teaching in the schools. These were, however, products of university courses with a mental-training plus literary criticism approach which left them uninformed about the foreign country and incapable in the oral language. The skills they had, though, fitted the examinations available, which were almost exclusively of the printed and written word. Inter-war textbooks might nod towards the Direct Method (and indeed one of the more popular ones, Mrs Saxelby's French Course[13], did a good deal more than nod) but classroom methods still consisted largely of: read aloud, translate into English, expound the grammar, write the test exercises, and, culmination, translate back into French.

The Second World War had an opposite effect to that of the First. Thanks largely to American military experience, new methods geared to new aims came to a post-war Britain that became more rapidly outward-looking than after World War One. In particular there had been a leap forward in technology. Wartime gramophones might be useful for playing records to the sixth form, but after the war the moveable, if not easily portable, tape-recorder and the reasonably reliable film-strip projector meant that a use-threshold of the technology had been crossed: it could be fitted by an enthusiastic teacher into her everyday teaching without too much difficulty. Just as important, a new theory of language learning and the course materials to go with it were there.

The new approach was based on behaviourist ideas of learning. These saw language — spoken language — as a collection of habits, and language teaching as habit formation. The amount of language to which the learner was exposed was to be strictly limited but unsimplified; real language with real intonation at real speed. It was to be 'over!~arned' by repetition so that it became automatic, and was not to be analysed grammatically (there was no grammar progression in the early courses) but manipulated by the substitution of items in 'open' slots in the utterance: *Je te l'ai déjà // envoyé/emprunté /donné . . . J'aurais bien voulu // des poires/une carte postale/un verre d'eau* . . . The tape-recorder was essential to provide the repeated models for pupil repetition. With only a tape-recorder the method was termed 'audio-lingual'; with the addition of film-strip still-pictures to give instant recognition of the 'meaning' of the utterance (i.e. the context in which it could be effectively uttered) the method became 'audio-visual'.

The TAVOR[14] course produced at SHAPE headquarters in Paris to teach French to non-French-speaking personnel of NATO forces was the first audio-visual course to become available in British schools, in the late 1950s. It was based on the behaviourist principles just stated, with language load very heavily reduced and overlearning through much repetition (each phrase was parroted three times) central to classroom work. It concentrated on spoken production of a limited but useful range of French, with stress on exact intonation, normal (or at least near-normal) speed, real French expressions (or so they appeared in comparison with what was otherwise available), and with no grammar progression or simplification of the language in the early stages of learning. By concentrating on a limited area of one skill and hammering this through new technology, the course appeared to work. The mind-numbing effect of the constant repetition was alleviated initially by the positive motivation produced by the novelty of the equipment: specially darkened rooms, tape-recorders, coloured cartoons projected on a screen. But whereas this was originally designed as material to be used in classrooms in Paris where the world of French culture began at the classroom door and where the French learned could be immediately applied just along the road to buy postcards or get a drink, in the English school situation this was not the case. Teachers mesmerized by the technology made little or no attempt to set up classroom situations where the overlearned structures might be needfully, autonomously used (this is the most difficult and often the most neglected part of foreign language teaching anyway). The accent, the speed, the intonation, the impressive Frenchness of the language learned were all there to prove that it worked (and were not these all areas that had so often been criticized in the past?). But, gradually it became clear that a year or longer spent on TAVOR (or the other basic audio-visual courses that followed it) meant little more than a command of only those snippets of language that had been overlearned in the classroom. There was no transfer, no ability to develop or recombine them, no ability to generate further language. A small part of the language-learning process involving often neglected skills had been concentrated on without the realization of *how* small a part this was and how much more there was to language teaching and learning than this; how much had in fact been neglected. Gradually this was realized and the audio-visual 'method' was dropped.[15]

Its demise was hastened by criticisms of the behaviourist learning theory that underpinned it. The central figure of behaviourist psychology in terms of its application to language learning was B. F. Skinner. From 1959 criticism of his work and theory by Noam Chomsky[16] and his followers produced an alternative approach that stressed language as rule-governed behaviour and suggested that the mechanism for formulation of these rules to generate 'new' language was a good deal more subtle than mere habit-formation. In teaching terms[17] this meant exposure to a great deal more of the language than the behaviourists were prepared to admit, much more opportunity for use by pupils of their own acquired store of the foreign language for purposes that they perceived as their own, and a view of error that saw it not as something to be avoided at all costs but as something to be learnt from, with fluency a higher good than accuracy.

A further technological 'breakthrough' of the late sixties was the language laboratory, seductive in its apparent individualization of learning and the consequent intensification of individual effort, and impressive as a status symbol, giving language teaching in the school something of the kudos of chemistry or physics. Again, apparently effective when the machinery was new and motivation high by reason of its novelty value, it proved inefficient, dehumanizing, and, as with the audio-visual course, led to concentration on one small formal aspect of language. Most of the work done in the laboratory was again based on the Skinnerian view of operant conditioning as basic to language learning, with overlearning of structures, this time through the four-phase drill, and again at the expense of the generation of personal language by the student. It proved to be an even more costly failure than the audio-visual 'method'.[18]

It is easy to be sceptical after the event, but the teachers who showered enthusiasm on the audio-visual method or the language laboratory were genuinely concerned to realign language teaching. There was, indeed still is, a feeling that society now requires school-taught language to be of some use in real transactions, that shortening lines of communication throughout the world should be accompanied by the learning of language for use rather than as 'mental discipline'. These teachers may have been infatuated with a device, deluded by 'experts', or taken in by the novelty effect of their new approach, but they were genuinely seeking to reorient classroom language teaching (and finding it more difficult than they expected). The primary school French movement (see Chapter 1) was another light that failed, another unsuccessful but nevertheless gallant attempt to turn language teaching towards new aims.

But out of all these apparent failures (and it should be stressed that none of them was a *total* failure), there has come one success at least. It has become clear that fascination with cleverly developed means is not a substitute for precise definition of ends, of a clear view of what 'foreign language learning' should represent for a particular child, both along the way in terms of his or her development and at the end in terms of what he or she is left with from the school foreign language classes on finally quitting them for good. Her Majesty's Inspectors in 1977, considering problems in modern languages, wrote of 'insufficiently differentiated objectives' and the need to 'offer pupils a terminal objective that they can perceive for themselves'.[19] In their report of the same year on modern languages in comprehensive schools they wrote 'Much of the underperformance revealed in this report results from a tacit assumption that all pupils studying a modern language have basically the same needs. It is abundantly clear, however, that such an assumption is not only false but has unfortunate, often distressing, consequences for many of them'.[20]

This is all part of a growing emphasis on specifying ends, of starting not from a theory of language learning that may well be superseded or drop from fashion, nor from innovations in means that appear to revolutionize teaching methods. Defined ends as the overriding factor, and means justified only in their effectiveness towards reaching these ends, correspond to the utilitarian spirit of the age. This is, for example, at the heart of the graded-objectives movement, which is concerned with ends rather than means and relies on eclecticism rather than fanaticism to achieve its ends.[21] But focusing on the specific ends in modern language teaching for individual learners inevitably raises questions of the role of language learning within the whole curriculum, both as this is provided overall by the school and as it is experienced individually by the various members of that school. This is what Chapter 3 now attempts to do.

Footnotes

[1] *Novissima linguarum methodus*, 1648, quoted in Jelinek V. ed. *The Analytic Didactic of Comenius* Chicago 1953.

[2] ibid.

[3] Kelly J. C. *25 Centuries of Language Teaching* Rowley, Mass. Newbury House 1969, p. 11.

[4] In England the watershed has been dated specifically to the Restoration

(1660), which brought a French-speaking court to this country and effectively finished Latin, already dying, as the language of scholars and diplomats.

[5] All of which sounds surprisingly like modern mentalist views of language acquisition. One of Noam Chomsky's more accessible and less well-known works is titled *Cartesian Linguistics*. Plus ça change . . .?

[6] *Orbis sensualium pictus* was reprinted in an English edition in 1887.

[7] Blackie J. S. *On the Studying and Teaching of Languages* Edinburgh 1852.

[8] With this emphasis it was usually called the Natural Method. Its main advocate was the Frenchman F. Gouin, whose *L'art d'enseigner* was published in 1880. Translated into English in 1892, the work had some impact in its plea for a return in second-language learning to methods a child employs in learning its first language. Sweet amongst others pointed out the fallacy in assuming that the adolescent or adult learning a second language starts from a similar position to the child learning its mother tongue. More recently McLaughlin has made clear that the impression that we learn our first language in about four years simply is not true. Verbal comprehension reaches 80% of adult competence only at age eighteen. (McLaughlin B. *Second Language Acquisition in Childhood* Hillsdale N. J. 1978) p. 55.

[9] Palmer H. E. *The Principles of Language Study* Harrap 1922, reissued O.U.P. 1964.

[10] Kelly L. G. op. cit. p. 62.

[11] Palmer H. E. op. cit. p. 113.

[12] Krashen S. *Second Language Acquisition and Second Language Learning* Pergamon 1981.

[13] Saxelby E. *Cours de Français* Ginn 1936. It included separately published phonetic transcripts of the texts.

[14] TAVOR is an acronym of Teachers' Audio-Visual Oral.

[15] It is instructive to compare the first and second versions of the first two years of the Longman Audio-Visual Course (Moore S. and Antrobus A. L. 1966 and 1973), the only audio-visual course that retained general popularity. Even in its first version the course represents a compromise with the pure audio-visual doctrine, but it does have the audio-visual element as the central and virtually exclusive element; the second version de-emphasizes it and adds many exercises aimed at stimulation of language-generation.

[16] Initially in Chomsky's article: 'Skinner's *Verbal Behaviour*' in *Language* 35,1 (1959).

[17] The mentalists were much more wary about the direct application of their language-learning theories to teaching than the behaviourists had been. None the less their ideas were adopted where their critiques seemed to correspond to classroom experience.

[18] See Green P. S. ed. *The Language Laboratory in School* Oliver and Boyd 1975 for an unambiguous account of the laboratory's lack of success with high ability boys: '(pupils using a language laboratory) showed no detectable difference over a period of three years, in either performance or attitude, from a matched group of pupils that did not use the language laboratory'. Winter R. in *The Effectiveness of the Language Laboratory in Mixed Ability Teaching in Schools* (unpub. Ph.D. thesis, University of Sheffield 1982) found it equally ineffectual with secondary beginners of both sexes across the ability range.

[19] *Maths, Science and Modern Languages in Maintained Schools in England* HMI 1977 p. 2.

[20] *Modern Languages in Comprehensive Schools* (HMI series: Matters for Discussion 3) HMSO 1977 p. 47.

²¹ Whether computer-assisted language learning is another blind alley concerned with means at the expense of ends it is still too early to say. Certainly there were many danger signals: in the early pioneering materials, mastery and use of the technology took precedence over what was being taught, and the aims and content of the material seemed to have little relative importance. But this could well be only a first stage of naïve enthusiasm. Certainly there is in the expanding capabilities of the microcomputer a huge technological potential that it should be possible to harness to some at least of modern language learning's current aims. See Davies G. and Higgins J. *Computers, language and language learning* CILT 1982.

3 Language learning in the school curriculum

The school curriculum may mean, in one definition, the total educational experience on offer in an institution: chemistry, the chess club, the skiing trip, even school dinners. It may mean, in another, more sinister definition, the organization of children to meet society's unexpressed norms, a hidden curriculum of social or political manipulation. In most public debate, however, curriculum means something more tangible: although it may be conceived in terms of areas of experience to be developed — the sensory, the moral, the aesthetic, the logical, the religious, and so on — it will be expressed in terms of subjects. Most of these subjects will have familiar names, because education is a conservative process with a vested interest in stability, and most changes that occur will be within a subject. Where new subjects appear — humanities, social studies, environmental studies — they tend to be defined originally in terms of the old subjects that contribute to them. Curriculum, the subject curriculum, is determined in the English secondary school by the head teacher, at any rate in theory.

In this sense, then, curriculum means the specific subjects that are on offer to specific pupils at specific ages. It presupposes questions like: what subjects should all pupils experience and for how long? Which subjects should be offered as options and should the choosing of a certain number of options be compulsory? What combinations of options are possible and desirable? How much of the school experience should be common to all pupils and how much should represent a free choice by the pupil of subjects that interest him? Should all or any of the content of a subject be the same for all pupils? Presumably our theoretical Head knows enough about the syllabus content of each individual subject as it is to be taught, to be able to offer both a wide enough *à la carte* menu to cater for all tastes in the areas where choice is involved, and a *prix fixe* menu or menus to provide a balanced educational diet in those areas where the curriculum is compulsory. This in turn presupposes an earlier stage of curriculum planning at which our headmaster has defined exactly what educational experiences are appropriate to specific children (or perhaps to all children) at particular stages of their development, and then considered which subjects, taught in which way and with what content-emphasis, are likely to produce those educational experiences, together with the appropriate balance between experiences. Is, for example, logical thinking a basic and universal aim? If so, which subject taught in which way would achieve this best? Would different subjects be more effective at different ages? Or for different ability levels? Or for girls rather than boys? Is logical thinking to be catered for through mathematics? Computer science? Latin? Modern languages taught by the Grammar-Translation method? Or by a special course in logical thinking?

Is development of an aesthetic sense also basic? Is this to be done through English, music, art, French literature? And at what levels? And can our Head be sure that, say, music is actually being taught in 3Z's classroom in such a way as to produce the development of an aesthetic sense? How do we get the balance right for each child? And are we sure that we know what is right for each child anyway?

The answer to this last question is clearly a political one. It can produce in national education systems, on the one hand the precise and unified curriculum of the Soviet school, with every child in principle being taught the same things in the same way to a clearly defined and overriding end, or on the other hand the supermarket approach of the American school with each child trundling his trolley round, accompanied by his guidance counsellor, picking up a can of Algebra I here, a packet of French II here, a half-credit box of Glee Club there until he has what he considers to be an appropriately nutritional educational meal for himself at his present age and stage of development.[1]

In the English system each Head will, in theory, define educational experiences he thinks pupils should have and then institute subjects, and specific syllabuses and methods within the subjects, which will give the pupils these experiences. He will allow the pupils (and their parents) some choice in this, but ultimately responsibility for the educational experience offered by his school rests with him. *L'école, c'est moi.* In theory.

In practice, the constraints are such that the model we have just described is usually invisible. To start with few head teachers set up a school *ab initio*. They inherit a going concern, and the most important fact about a going concern is that it is going, functioning. It is relatively easy to tackle those parts which are functioning inefficiently and reorganize them, but to change those that are doing their job well, because the job appears to the Head to be unnecessary or wrongly directed, is an extremely difficult task. Most Heads ultimately settle for tinkering with the machine to make it function more smoothly. For example, here are Her Majesty's Inspectors reporting on not untypical curriculum practice in the first three years of secondary schooling:

> One comprehensive school in a poor area is well satisfied with its traditional organization and curriculum. The common course comprises the traditional subjects, there is no experiment in integrated studies, and innovations such as computer studies and control technology are left to a later stage. The policy of the headmaster is to make haste slowly in order to carry parents, pupils and staff along at a pace they can tolerate. He would like to experiment with combined studies and with new patterns of teacher co-operation because he believes that the curriculum might gain in meaning and richness and the teaching in variety and quality. But by innovating judiciously, he tempers idealism and ambition with realism and common sense: the curriculum suits the pupils because it matches their expectations.'[2]

Even where a Head has the chance to start a new school and construct its curriculum, the 'educational experiences' approach will provide no more than a rough check on subject balance. There are external constraints that push the Head into producing a subject menu not unlike the one offered by the institution down the road. A Head who, for instance, decided to ignore first-year mathematics in favour of a course in logical thinking would rapidly find himself in trouble from parents, governors, LEA, and possibly the local newspaper. When a Head inherits a school, as he usually does, he inherits subject teachers, Heads of Department, existing subject syllabuses, traditional balances between subjects, established pupil and parent expectations. He will influence all of these to a greater or lesser extent, partly on the basis of his own curricular philosophy, but much more to provide rapid resolutions of pressing everyday problems. Problems like, who do we replace, a retiring art teacher or a retiring Germanist, where only one replacement is possible? Such matters are more commonly decided on grounds such as 'Can Mrs Jones who has a joint honours degree take on some German as well as her French?' rather than on a judicious consideration of the comparative weightings of each subject in terms of aesthetic development and language education within the curriculum as a whole.

What is our imaginary Head likely to inherit in a typical modern languages department? He will have a staff largely teaching French, not all of whom are highly qualified to teach it. Most of the younger staff will have been trained to teach a foreign language, will have a degree in one or two languages, some of them having followed courses in the newer universities that stress language and civilization rather than literature, and almost all of them will have spent a year abroad (though not necessarily in France). These younger staff will have been trained to teach in comprehensive schools and most will have gained all their teaching experience in comprehensive schools. The older staff will have a different background. Many will have trained and gained their early experiences in grammar schools, at a time when little modern languages teaching took place outside the grammar school, and will have taught successfully for some years of their early careers in a fairly academic atmosphere to fairly academic pupils. Their own first degree will be on average less language-oriented than those of their younger colleagues and a number of them will not have spent a year abroad. Most will by now have adapted to the demands of the comprehensive school and to teaching across the ability range, at any rate at some levels within the school, most will have made up over the years for the lack of oral emphasis in their own language education, most will travel frequently in France or Germany. But not all. Our imaginary Head will certainly inherit some teachers whose own spoken French (even if it is their first foreign language) is not up to the demands of oral teaching at some levels, whose sympathies do not entirely lie with teaching languages to the less able, whose visits to France are few and whose knowledge of the country is less than up-to-date. And among his French teaching staff he will certainly have some for whom French is a second or even third foreign language, whose oral competence is limited (even if the limits are well disguised), whose visits to the country are extremely infrequent and whose knowledge of it is superficial and dated. Teachers of French who, most importantly, are not greatly in sympathy with France or even find it and its people antipathetic. The methods of both these types of less-committed teacher will be as efficient as they can make them, but their aims will be limited by their ability to achieve them. The educational experience that a pupil gets from a slot in the timetable labelled 'French' from such a teacher may be radically different from that provided by a younger, more enthusiastic member of staff trained and working in a different tradition.

So to define exactly what educational contribution members of his modern languages staff may bring to an individual pupil's over-all experience will not be easy for a Head. He will rely, must rely, on his Head of Modern Languages to make sure that something of the curricular experience intended is passed on to the pupil. The crucial role of the Head of Department has been stressed in many reports. Indeed, only he can begin to monitor any individual's experience in modern languages classes, compare it with the experience intended, and initiate necessary, possible changes in the methods and attitudes of that pupil's teacher. 'Experience during the survey makes HM Inspectors more than ever convinced that the Head of Department is a key figure, the most important single factor governing the quality of language work in a school. His effectiveness is seen above all in the help and guidance which he gives to his colleagues.'[3]

The Head's role must be to integrate the Head of Modern Languages' syllabus, overall and as it affects individual pupils, into the school's entire curriculum on the one hand and into each pupil's own programme on the other. At a theoretical level this may mean considering what language-learning experiences are proposed in English for the second forms, considering where these are paralleled by French, and if necessary attempting to get the two departments to think in non-conflicting ways. At a practical everyday level it may mean realizing that 2C's French next term is largely based on a civilization project on the Camargue, that their geography work is on swamplands, and that integration is necessary if the same ground is not to be squelched over twice. Many Heads would not feel that the latter detail of everyday work is a part of their province, and in a large school it may well be a task allocated to the Director of Studies, the Head of Lower School, the Head of Middle School, etc. But it can all too easily end up as no one's task.

The direction in which the Head decides to influence language teaching will in part be determined by his views of what foreign language learning has to contribute generally to every child in terms of language and cultural experiences that, say, English and geography cannot, and what opportunities for longer-term language learning for mastery should be offered in the light of the likely take-up of options by pupils and the availability of staff. For intrinsic or (more often) extrinsic reasons, most Heads appear ultimately to decide that foreign-language learning experience for all has a clear contribution to make to the overall curriculum for the first two or three years and that one foreign language at least should be offered as an option beyond that. Where more than this is offered it is usually (though not always) because, as the National Association of Languages Advisers says, 'the early stages of the evolution of the comprehensive school have been marked by a determination. . .to maintain the curricular provision of the grammar schools' and thus 'foreign language teaching has passed almost intact into the reorganized schools'.[4] And in this latter sort of school it may well be that the foreign language provision has never been thought through at all in terms of its contribution to the individual's curriculum. Much individual disaffection and many classroom problems for the teacher stem directly from a pupil's quite legitimate question: 'what's the point of this *for me?*', 'this' being long-term language taught without the pupil's long-term commitment ('I'm giving this lot up next year, miss!').

However, given that language teaching *has* been organized in such a way as to provide a compulsory language-learning experience[5] for all, together with optional long courses for 'mastery' for some, the Head should find that the former course is making a considerable number of contributions to his pupils' overall curriculum experience, and not just in the area of language development.

Among these contributions he may find, firstly, the development of oral dexterity and an increased awareness of and sensitivity to speech systems other than the mother-dialect. This may be particularly important where, as is often the case, the pupil is *only* a dialect speaker. The ability to empathize with speakers of other languages or dialects is an important outcome of foreign language learning, and this in turn may have a positive effect in a mixed-race community in enabling the pupil to place himself imaginatively in another race's social position.

Secondly, the experience of learning a second language should help in the divorce of the English word from the object represented, in the realization that there are ways of organizing experience in terms of language other than the one that he has so far employed. To get beyond the stage of 'Miss, the French call it a chien, but it's a dog really, isn't it?' is to break down linguistic chauvinism and extend the boundaries of language in a way that will have a positive, derestricting effect on the pupil's perception of English as well.

Thirdly, cultural chauvinism is brought into question. The pupil may in his language-experience classes be brought for the first time to examine assumptions about what is normal (or natural) in terms of food and the way it is eaten, sports and why they are played or watched, music, holidays, the way a family spends its money and the relative importance attached to various items of the family budget, relationships within the family and their importance, friendships and sexual relationships and the assumptions and signals that go with them, religious beliefs and observances. In this respect the slot on the timetable labelled 'French' may, effectively taught, cover a whole range of genuinely educational experiences.

Fourthly, actual chauvinism should be modified by a view of another country that incorporates an ability to function, in however restricted a way, in something so intimate as its language. An approach to France via French, sensitively done, involves something much more personal for the pupil than the facts and ideas of a geography lesson; if he wishes to, he can keep his geography at a much less involved, much more academically impersonal level. Learning French is a step, perhaps small, towards making him a citizen of the world rather than of Barnsley.

Finally he may find that the pupil in these classes gets some initial ideas of language generalization, of how language works. As he learns even the smallest amount of French, the pupil realizes that there are aspects of language that are apparently generalizable (at any rate between these two, his mother tongue and French) and others that are not. Some overt analysis and comparison of the two languages will undoubtedly take place, and this is something that the pupil will not normally get from his English course alone, on whatever principles it is organized. The beginning of a broader view of what languages *are* is, here, useful undoubtedly if he eventually comes to learn a foreign language for mastery, but also a valuable perception in its own right.

The Head of Modern Languages might wish to make yet further claims in support of the curricular contribution of a language-experience course for all, but the Head may well feel that the above are sufficient to justify a self-contained two-year language-experience course provided it is properly organized and taught. We shall turn to just such practicalities in the next chapter. The Head, meanwhile, may be turning a beady eye on the long-course language option or options. Language for mastery. It sounds good, but what exactly does it mean? And what is its curriculum contribution?

Such a course needs to be more or less self-contained in three years. It is true that it will have attitudes and ideas from the general language experience course to build on, and if the mastery course is in French, rather than some other language, some basic French language as well. It is also true that some, a minority, of the pupils may be expected to continue to study the language after 16+. But the only safe view of the course is as a three-year, self-contained block. Not even that if the Head decides that a language option is not available until the fourth year, for then the additional third year of the language-experience course will have to serve, uneasily and perhaps ineffectually, as final, culminating year for those not continuing with the French option, and as initial year of the mastery course. Not an easily workable combination.

What then is the curricular contribution of the language mastery course? In purely developmental terms, many of the arguments for the language-experience course continue to apply here, and in greater depth. The second language should now become a part of the pupil's mental make-up, with some real attempt at thinking in the language, and genuine self-expression. It should take him far enough to feel that he has another 'French' self who behaves differently, linguistically, culturally, socially, from his English self. Certainly not at this stage, if ever, as a Frenchman, but with a growing Frenchness. It is this development of the other, quasi-French self that is the most liberating thing about learning a language in depth. And the pupil who has pursued a mastery course should also be able to turn back on his English with the necessary distancing for critical appraisal of his mother tongue, its use, its precision or lack of precision, its meaning, and of his English culture, its strengths and weaknesses.

Secondly, any subject chosen as an option may have an instrumental value for the chooser. It may be seen as valuable either for work or leisure. The value of a language for leisure, if taught in a communicative way, is self-evident, though the languages of the less accessible countries are at something of a disadvantage here. In vocational terms the usefulness of languages in many jobs as an adjunct to other skills is clear. Their necessity for exporting industry has been stated time and again, from 1930:

> 'In almost all markets it is a damaging, and often a fatal, handicap if representatives, whether principals or subordinates, cannot converse freely with the customer in his own language as well as read his newspapers and trade journals.'[6]

to 1979:

> 'The days when English-speaking markets took the bulk of British exports are over . . . Linguistic ability will not only save time and expense. It will also make it easier for the exporter to build up an effective rapport with his customer. In many competitive industries this is likely to make the difference between a contract won and a contract lost.'[7]

It is clear, however, that industry is not interested in linguists *per se*, however much it sees languages as a valuable additional asset.[8] It is true, too, that in spite of our closer ties with Europe, for most pupils who continue a language to 16+ this will have no direct job application. None the less, the option-chooser may reasonably see more utilitarian possibilities, in both leisure and work, in the choice of a foreign language than in that of many other subject options on offer.⁹

So including one or more foreign languages among his option choices at this level, our Head may well feel justified in terms both of a pupil's personal educational development and the additional usable skill to be gained from the course. But again, for these curricular ends to be achieved, the means used must be appropriate. Unless the course has communicative objectives, most of the ends seen above as desirable will not be reached. And our Head would be wise not to treat success at O level in languages as evidence of the ends being attained, but to consider the intentions, methods, work programme, and balance of skills of the actual course in relation to its intended curricular contribution.

Finally we must consider the curricular role of foreign languages in school beyond the age of 16. It is here that least progress has been made, where the inclusion of many of the existing type of A-level courses, even as an option, is becoming ever more difficult to justify, where competition from outside the school first effectively appears, and where pupils are most easily able to vote with their feet and are doing so.

The traditional sixth-form course leading to A level at its most old-fashioned is the last refuge of the Grammar-Translation method. Here the grammar book and the prose reign, the study of literature means line-by-line translation, and spoken French is a rarity. Such courses when well taught within their own terms remain acceptable to a small minority of students, in practice almost entirely girls, who see them as a way to A level and university studies, not necessarily in languages, and who treat them at the level of superior crossword-puzzle problems. They are increasingly unacceptable both to students who *can* cope with them, but require something else, an extension of the communicative courses they have experienced lower down the school, and also to students who *cannot* cope, who are in the sixth form with quite mixed motivation and whose language abilities are varied. The latter students in the past would have left at sixteen and taken jobs which now no longer exist for them. They are not uninterested or ungifted in languages: by definition they are not pre-sixteen language dropouts. But they are certainly not candidates for a traditional A-level syllabus. Nor are they easy students for the staff they are likely to meet on such courses. For it is here that our Head meets his most intractable problem. It is in this academic niche that many of his older, ex-grammar school staff spend a good deal of their time. The traditional sixth-form course corresponds to their skills: to have to teach for communication in the spoken language, for knowledge of France, for aural competence *at a sixth-form level* is beyond their abilities. To point to examination success in the A levels that correspond to their courses is no answer when overall numbers actually taking A level as it stands continue steadily to fall.[10]

The Head will have to grasp this nettle, for clearly all the arguments for the 16+ course apply even more strongly here. Properly taught, a sixth-form student can begin to feel *genuine* mastery, to conceive of her 'French' self as real and separate, to feel more and more at home in the foreign culture, and at the same time rejoice in the manipulation of her foreign language as a genuinely useful tool. It has become a valuable way of continuing her education on her own, a tool for self-generated development. But it will not be easy for the Head to ensure that his sixth-form course is taught in such a way as to provide this.

The other stumbling blocks apart from staff are the A-level syllabuses and the demands of the universities. New syllabuses are, however, appearing[11], some of the older universities are rethinking their courses to give them greater communicative emphasis, and most of the newer universities have always had modern language courses in which communicative skills were paramount. To justify a place in the school curriculum for modern languages at sixth-form level they must be seen as an extension of the 13–16 'mastery' course, with similar aims and values: all too often at the moment there is a lurch into old, unconsidered ways after O level that produces confusion, disappointment, and resentment in many pupils.

Let us suppose, however, that ends have been defined at each stage, that the curricular contributions that language learning *can* make, defined above, have been accepted as desirable, that courses are organized to ends appropriate to the pupils following them. What should be the content of such courses, and what techniques and materials are available and effective in teaching them? It is with these and related questions, the nuts and bolts of foreign language teaching, that Part II of this book deals.

Footnotes

[1] Neither system works out quite so simply in practice, but these are the principles implied.
[2] DES *Ten Good Schools: A Secondary Schools Enquiry* HMSO 1977.
[3] *Modern Languages in Comprehensive Schools* (op. cit.) p. 19.

National Association of Language Advisers *Foreign Languages in Schools* (no date: late 1970s).

⁵ One should distinguish language-experience courses from language-awareness courses. Central to the former is the actual learning of a language in some, at any rate, of its aspects. Language-awareness courses concentrate on the functions and relationships of language, both as an area of knowledge valuable in itself and as a preparation for future foreign language learning.

⁶ Board of Education *Report of Committee on Education for Salesmanship* 1930.

⁷ British Overseas Trade Board *Foreign Languages for Overseas Trade* 1979.

⁸ See, for instance, Emmans K. A. *et al. Foreign Languages in Industry and Commerce* University of York 1974.

⁹ There is, of course, the intrinsic interest of the subject for the learner as a further motive for choice, as with all subjects on offer. The language-experience course has therefore additional importance as a taster course for the language option.

¹⁰ The percentage of school leavers attempting A-Level French in 1970–71 was: Boys 2.3%, Girls 4.4%. In 1980–81 it was: Boys 1.4%, Girls 4.1%.

¹¹ See, for instance, *French 16–19: a New Perspective* (Report of the French 16–19 Study Group) Hodder 1981. This proposes a new communicative syllabus and assessment procedure for students who would at the moment be capable of reaching A level in French.

Part II
Means

4 The language-experience course

We will start then by assuming that a discrete two-year course exists or can be organized. Even if our school is organized simply on the old five-year course basis, in practical terms, if we are prepared to recognize it, we are offering a two- or three-year course to more than half our pupils, since after that, at the point of option, most of them will opt out. Perhaps if we treat the first two years in a more self-contained way, fewer *will* opt out.

We have seen in Chapter 3 what we might expect the pupils to get from these two years in terms of general educational objectives, but what exactly should they also be able to do at the end? It is easier to answer the first point than the second. The curriculum contributions of the course that were discussed in Chapter 3 can be summed up, from a pupil's point of view, as: a sense of linguistic achievement, the feeling of burrowing our way into the foreign environment via the language, the feeling that the environment is no longer foreign, no longer 'out there', but that it forms to some extent part of us, that we represent 'France' (or 'Germany', or whatever country), that we have a touch of Frenchness in our make-up, however slight, for people who have not. That we are a little closer to a different culture, and so the world is a little smaller. That we can cross the Channel, and though they will still be Frogs, the word will have a little love attached to it: it will be affectionate rather than dismissive. Once there we shall be prepared to chance our arm with what we have learned, to help us in our everyday life, and be secretly rather pleased when we understand them and they understand us, when the words produce the wine. We should end the course a bigger person with more possibilities and more doors open to us.

The second, more difficult, question, 'What should we be able to do?', involves the matter of ability. In two years, however organized, some children will learn more than others (and if this is not the case we ought to be asking ourselves whether we are unwittingly holding some children back): this is fine for them and need not prevent our aims being achieved. For instance, the words-into-wine effect is the same, as an effect, whether the words are '*un verre de vin rouge*' or '*je ne sais pas exactement, je crois que je vais prendre une bière — non, non, plutôt du vin rouge, oui, oui, un verre de vin rouge*'. If classes are organized on a mixed-ability basis, this means working around topics which the more able will treat in more detail; if classes are setted (and this is still the more common pattern even at the 11+, 12+ level we are speaking of) and teaching is more linear, it means ensuring that the lines are all going via the same place (and that it *is* a place, that there is a destination and those leaving the train are not just getting off in the middle of the countryside).

All this means thinking the course backwards from its end. That end, in any basic course that purports to teach children to communicate in a foreign language, should surely be an opportunity for all to communicate in the foreign country, to measure the effectiveness of their classroom learning against its usefulness in the country. This means, as an end to the basic course, in both senses of the word 'end', a properly organized, productive visit to France of, we would suggest, several days and if possible, at least a week. The course that leads to this will be determined by what is possible logistically on the visit and where it is to be. But assuming the course is to be organized by topics, all pupils at the end might be expected to do, with varying fluency, things like the following:

Topic: **Transport**
- Knowing how the local transport system works.
- Having the necessary language to buy and cope with a ticket (in this sort of approach words like *composter* in French become important recognition vocabulary).
- Being able to understand notices and route maps.
- Being able to ask for and cope with interchange tickets.
- Having the necessary language to cope with obvious emergencies (Am I on the right tram? Does this one go as far as Uccle? Has the last bus gone yet?).

Topic: **Buying drinks**
- Knowing what sort of drinks are available and where.
- Knowing what prices are likely to be.
- Being aware of the current paying/tipping system.
- Knowing the necessary social mores (Are alcoholic drinks served to children? What food is likely to be available? Are prices different in different parts of the café or bar?)
- Having the necessary language to ask for and pay for drinks.
- Being able to understand the waiter's most likely questions.[1]
- Being able to read the officially posted price-list, if there is one.
- Being able to read the handwritten figures of a bill or the

printed figures of a pay-chit (and incidentally having sufficient arithmetic to check it!)

Topic: **Buying food in a restaurant**
- Knowing the necessary eating mores (spotting restaurant levels, recognizing a self-service restaurant, finding and judging a menu beforehand, knowing the sequence of courses and use of cutlery, tipping).
- Having the necessary language to read the menu (as with the waiter, at the lowest level of ability this simply means recognizing one or two favourite dishes — *biftek pommes frites* perhaps — but much more for the able child), knowing the standard menu phrases (*prix fixe, service inclus, menu à . . .*, etc.), having sufficient language to cope with the drinks section.
- Being able to produce the spoken French for an order, and to be able to read aloud simple known noun items (and, for the more able, unknown items as well).
- Being able to make a further order and eventually to pay the bill.
- As in the café, being able to read and understand a handwritten bill.[2]

Topic: **Buying presents**
- Using and understanding basic shop arrival and departure exchanges.
- Using *Je voudrais* . . . and expressions of liking and disliking.
- Suggesting change of colour, size, material, price.
- Saying you will/will not buy, and if necessary apologizing.
- Being able to manipulate money, amounts and change.

Topic: **Television**[3]
- Understanding *Télé-7-Jours* for programme gist.
- Asking to, and how to, switch on/off, change channel, turn sound up/down, all within the superpolite framework necessary for a 12-year-old to get these things done.
- Understanding the gist of announcers' standard jargon. Clearly at this level not much of the programmes themselves will be understood, though something like Fawlty Towers dubbed into French, or French weather forecasts or news will produce some gist understanding. The latter can be incorporated into the course via videos made by French friends or the assistant.

Topic: **Getting to know someone**
This topic supposes that pupils will want to talk at a more

personal level than the above topics assume, to someone French, especially of their own age.
- Describing oneself, one's house, one's town, one's school, one's interests.
- Asking questions of the interlocutor in the same areas.
- Asking for elucidation (questions and expressions like: *je ne comprends pas exactement* . . ., *qu'est-ce qu'un* . . .?, *qui est* . . .?, *qu'est-ce que tu as (vous avez) dit?*).

And so on; this list of topics is of course not exhaustive.

The last topic, involving the social point of *tu as/vous avez,* brings us back to the question of grammar and vocabulary sequencing, indeed the whole organization of the course that is leading to the ability to function in the areas listed above. It needs to be made clear that it does not *just* lead to this, that the knowledge of France and the French gained should help cope with what is met on the visit, but that the course is not simply preparation for one visit, and equally will by no means prepare for all eventualities on any visit. We also need to consider whether the success in getting the wine, finding the métro, eating a meal, being chatted up (and understanding it) by a French lad is enough, or whether there should be some organized account of the degree of success in each topic area. A diary of the visit can provide this: we shall return to this point. Let us first consider the organization of a two-year course with these objectives.

A course of this kind naturally lends itself to classroom simulations of situations as the starting point. Each situation will involve background explanation, exploration of French/British differences and similarities, use of photos, realia, maybe TV and videotape; it will mean looking at language functions (how do we say hello, goodbye, apologize, ask for things, compare things, enthuse, express polite dislike, express regret, ask for something to be repeated, ask for something to be done . . .?) It will group much of its vocabulary by centres of interest. It will also (and some early course-writers in this area have been reluctant to admit this) mean grammatical explanations of the language met. This will not be linear grammar of the kind that, in the author's opinion, is still the most fruitful way of organizing a mastery course. It will be explanatory grammar arising from a need to come to grips with language in a specific context. For example:

un verre de . . . } The concept of gender in French needs
une tasse de . . . } explaining. Examples can be taken from German, Italian, Spanish to show that French

	is normal in this respect and that English is the odd one out.
tu as dit?	The past tense — how the French say things in the past — is seen to be equivalent to one of our past tenses, but we don't use them the same way. Very many children of this age will not have noticed a difference in English between *you've said* and *you said*. Here as elsewhere judicious grammar explanation of 'the French we've just been using' also enlightens, clarifies, makes more precise the way the English we've been using for years is organized.
je comprends *je ne comprends pas* *je l'aime* *je ne l'aime pas*	Word order in French: we need to stress the importance, in listening to French, of concentrating on that spot between subject and verb which gives you information you'd find after the verb in English.

The pupil will not of course know thoroughly the sequence of grammar topics that would be covered in the first two books of a five-year course, but he will know sufficient to explain the useful material he learned within his situational work, and the grammar will be functional enough for him to expand this material somewhat further so that it does not remain as inert phrases but is usable. The fact that all the grammar the pupil learns must derive from situations prevents the teacher falling into the trap of teaching sterile grammatical material.[4]

The result of a course organized in this way will not be a pupil who is a fluent speaker or a precise understander, and we should not pretend that it will. Two years, after all, is only about eighty hours of class time. What the pupil has learned, however, will be useful in itself and a foundation in all sorts of ways for a 'mastery' course if he then opts to go on to this. Amongst other things it gives that splendidly motivational lift: 'Yes, I recognize that — we met that already last year — that's where that fits in . . . .'

A syllabus such as the one suggested above lies at the centre of many modern situation-based textbook-plus-tape courses that aim at giving some experience of language learning to all. Whether the teacher starts from such a course or produces her own materials, she will rapidly realize that useful situations *in themselves* have only a limited motivational power with eleven- or twelve-year-olds. It is no more possible just to 'follow the book' and hope to hold the children with a modern course of this kind than it was a generation ago with, say, *Cours Illustré* or two generations ago with *Whitmarsh's First French Book*. If the eleven- or twelve-year-old is to make the language learnt his own, he must first see that it is really made for him. And this means, for even the busiest or least imaginative or laziest teacher, some attempt to produce presentation materials that tailor the language (or appear to) specially to little Kevin in the back row, and then to go on to devise class situations where Kevin will really *want* to use it.

But before we go on to look in more detail at how the material may be taught, let us first establish the three basic stages of teaching consequent on any given language input.

However language teaching material is organized it will involve a certain number of 'chunks' of input French. Each chunk of new material, whether spoken or printed, whether narrative prose or dialogue, whether organized around a situation, a function, a grammar point, or a language area (e.g. telling the time, colours, weather), will, as a first stage, have to be presented to the pupils, and the pupils will have to understand it.

The audio-visual 'method' often lost sight of this last point. Half-understood material leaves pupils puzzled, worried, resentful and unconfident. The feeling that meaningless sounds are being produced and that one is supposed to learn them can lead, at worst, to anxiety and fear.[5] So the first stage is presentation and comprehension of new material, probably embedded in a good deal of known material, and understanding of this by the pupils.

The second stage is the reproduction of the new material by the pupils in a controlled way determined by the teacher. At its simplest this is repetition of the input: beyond that it will involve some sort of manipulation of the input by the pupil, its extension to different situations or its change by slot substitution. This is the point where the drills of the audio-lingual approach can sometimes be valuable. At this stage the pupil is committing to memory, practising, and 'loosening up' the input material, or more precisely those parts of it the teacher wants the pupil to have as part of his actively-producible language. This is the language *practice* stage.

The third stage, still so often dreadfully neglected, involves arranging things so that the pupil uses the new material, together with old previously known material that he has already made his own, in ways *of his own*. This means inventing situations where the pupil feels he absolutely must *use*, for some vital purpose, language that until now he has only practised. For instance, 'Mais non, c'est à moi!' to get back the sweet that the teacher has filched and is about to eat or to give to a neighbour. From the teacher's point of view the pupil is using a newly-learned disjunctive pronoun. From the pupil's he is getting his property back. Attention is focused on the message, not the medium, but the imperative nature of the message means that the medium is used in a thought-less way. The fact that the pupil sometimes gets it wrong (in practice the above quite often appears as 'Mais non, c'est moi!') is of far less importance in this third stage than the fact that the pupil is using his own French for his own ends. The errors will be limited in any case if the second stage has been done efficiently.

In practice, of course, there will be overlap between the stages, there will be returning for revision from one stage to an earlier one, but all three stages need to be there and none of them can be missed out. Let us consider how each of them applies in practice in our two-year course, starting with presentation.

In these early stages the initial presentation of material orally is important for two reasons. Firstly, it establishes the oral form as the predominant one in the learner's mind. There is no doubt that, in addition to all the curricular aims of the language-experience course, spoken language, for both comprehension and production, will be dominant. Secondly, it avoids the problems of printed-word correspondence. With a language as unphonetic as French this is a considerable stumbling block, but even with the much more phonetic Spanish, Italian, or German, there are difficulties with the less able child. He may well have only recently established a tolerable relationship between the spoken and printed forms of his own language, and at eleven even the more able children are still having difficulties with fluency and accuracy when performing in written English. This is not, however, a plea for the banishment of the printed word. For some children the printed word is a necessary crutch for retaining the spoken form[6]; being able to see the printed form as well as hear the spoken one helps fix the spoken form in the mind. This needs to be set against the interference to accurate pronunciation produced by too much viewing of the printed word, and the danger, if the learner too often sees and hears material at the same time, of relying on the double input. One of the greatest problems of decoding a purely spoken message is deciding where the words begin and end: the written form solves this at a glance. [sɛlsɛl] said by a Frenchman is very difficult for a beginner to decipher orally, even if the Englishman has what he thinks is a pepper-pot in his hand, whereas the printed form *c'est le sel* by distinguishing the words leaves only one minor problem of vocabulary to resolve. The crutch of the printed word can be valuable, but it needs to be removed for much of the time if the learner is to walk in French on two legs.

So, we assume presentation via the spoken word and the use of the printed form as explanation and reinforcement, with not too much of it, but no *a priori* ban on seeing printed forms either. How are we then to present the spoken word? In practice the choice comes down to the teacher, the assistant (with or without the teacher), the tape-recorder and the video-recorder. The tape-recorder, reel-to-reel or cassette, has its value. Authentic French voices are a more accurate model, especially for intonation, than most teachers' own voices. But recorded voices are inflexible, and the quality of reproduction almost always leaves a lot to be desired. Classrooms are reverberant, tape-recorders' heads get clogged, loudspeakers are rarely of good enough quality, tone controls get left at 'bass' with the treble cut back. It is rare, as a visitor to modern languages classrooms, to hear a tape-recorder producing a really good model for children to imitate. Often the regular teacher, who has got used to the tape, the quality of reproduction, the reverberance of the classroom, does not notice this. The learner, coming to the material for the first time, does. One of the clearest findings of Burstall[7] was that pupils overwhelmingly found it more difficult to understand tape-recorder than teacher and preferred the latter. A good rule of thumb for the teacher seems to be: if in any doubt, repeat what the tape said; if in frequent doubt, scrap the tape and do it yourself. The latter course *does* pose problems if what is being presented is dialogue rather than narrative, but it is here that the assistant may be used. Assistants, where schools have them, are often pre-empted for sixth-form work. This can be a mistake, since in fact the assistant is of tremendous value, properly used and controlled, from the very beginning of language learning. The assistant can, for instance, be of great help in sharing the work of exploitation of material in stages two and three; here, at this first, presentation stage, the teacher plus the assistant can present dialogues with the added visual reality of gesture, movement, facial expression, reaction which the audio tape is incapable of. By offering the possibility of real dialogue in the classroom the assistant gives presentation an additional dimension. Our fourth mode of presentation, video, does, it is true, also have most of these advantages, and it combines them with a reality of setting and properties that cannot be achieved in the classroom. It still suffers from doubtful sound quality at times, and from the same artificialness that audio has. In a teacher/assistant dialogue the pupil knows that he may have to interact, in a moment, directly with one of the two participants. He knows he will not have to interact with a television screen.[8] So central to presentation should be teacher (assuming the teacher is capable!) or teacher plus assistant, with audio and video-tapes used occasionally to give all-important variety, and with the best reproductive equipment available.

Intimately connected with presentation, as we have seen, is clarification of meaning. There was little problem here for the old Grammar-Translation approach. Translation of the text clarified meaning, and country-specific material tended to be avoided (historically, this was because the method, as we have seen, had its origins in attempts at language generalization, with interest centring on what languages had in common rather than on distinguishing idiosyncrasies; more recently it was more due to a lack of knowledge of, or interest in, the country itself on the part of teachers and course-writers). Meaning could thus easily be carried by a parallel English text. Direct Method and the earlier audio-visual courses both refused to allow the English language into the classroom. Direct Method in particular evolved a whole range of strategies for the direct conveying of meaning, via objects, mime, visuals such as posters, flashcards, cut-outs, recontextualization (putting a word into a different, easier context or contexts), definition . . . Most of these have been adopted by teachers using other methods, because they proved effective. Of the strategies mentioned, the use of actual objects, their pictorial representation where the actual object is not available, and demonstration and mime using these objects are the most readily available at the level of which we are speaking. Their value in the learning process lies in vividness of association. A learner who is taught *C'est un chien* whilst a large labrador places its paws on his shoulders and licks his face is less likely to forget *chien* than one who has learned 'the dog' = *le chien*. *Nihil in intellectu quod non fuit prius in sensu,* said Aristotle, and Comenius quoted him approvingly.[9] It seems clear, at any rate at a basic level, that the more we can create this sort of direct *sensory* association with the verbal meaning, the more effective the teaching will be. So that, generally speaking, objects are more effective than pictures, and if we are teaching *une voiture* the learner will be helped if he holds as well as sees the toy car that determines meaning, if we are teaching *un bonbon* he will retain the word more effectively if he is allowed to eat as well as see the Smartie. Again, the magazine photo, pasted on card

57

and cut out to its outlines, that the pupil can handle, is slightly more effective than the picture, be it flashcard or filmstrip frame, that is simply shown to him from the front of the class. These in turn will be more effective than an English translation simply given to him. But in all this there must be one overriding consideration: the meaning must be clear and unambiguous. Here overlap between the first stage (presentation) and controlled reproduction will help, since answers to questions entailing reproduction may show up meaning problems: but they *may* not. Alternative demonstrations help, too. *Voiture* plus a photograph of a car could equal 'photograph'; *voiture* plus a toy car could equal 'toy', but both in succession make it quite clear that *voiture* equals 'car'. Or do they? Is there someone in the class who thinks that *voiture* equals 'violet' since both cars are this colour? If there is any doubt of this kind it seems entirely legitimate to check by pupil translation into English after having established the direct association of object and noun (or action and verb, or flashcard and adjective, etc.) and, perhaps, the beginnings of repetition-practice.

English seems legitimate, too, for items not readily converted into sense images (visual, auditory, even gustatory), such words as *déjà, beaucoup, cependant* that have meanings difficult to present unambiguously. But the overall principle is clear: as much foreign language as possible in the classroom presentation consistent with clarity of understanding.[10]

It need hardly be said that this sort of approach, provided the pupils *are* absolutely clear about meaning, also makes learning more fun. It allows for far more variety, makes the language lesson one in which the unexpected regularly happens, and incidentally ties French directly to the world about them rather than simply leaving it as an intellectual abstraction (an important point in the light of the level of development that an 11+ class has normally reached).

The second stage of the language-teaching process is the teacher-controlled reproduction of the new material. This second stage must overlap with the first. A new dialogue or piece of narrative may be read by the teacher or the tape played through *in toto* to start with, but as it is repeated section by section (or sentence by sentence) and meaning made clear, the first stage of reproduction, repetition, needs to be built in. Language heard and not produced, at this early stage when so much is new, will not stick. Worse, the student feels frustrated, anxious, even angry if he is not allowed to attempt to fix what he hears by saying it. The next stage downhill is the glassy stare and the internal switch-off to modern languages entirely. Chorus work needs therefore to be built in at this stage: it is vital psychologically even if it is less than totally effective methodologically. In terms of method it presents control problems (Is everyone repeating? Are they all repeating accurately?), intonation problems (It's getting flatter, it's getting slower), and problems of boredom (Here we go again, another chorus, all on the same note . . .). All can be alleviated by the teacher being demanding in terms of pace and volume, and by varying full chorus with half chorus (left versus right, front versus back), single rows, individuals, or regularly organized teams (*les crocodiles* versus *les chameaux*). Indeed, since each phrase or sentence will need to be repeated half a dozen times or so for it to begin to stick, this sort of variation is vital. Use of individuals among the various choruses is naturally important, too: it gives valuable feedback to see how well the phrase is being learned by specific individuals ('she's quick, she'll help provide a model; if *he's* got it they've all got it!') and it also allows a direct check on those suspected of hiding in the chorus. Equally the various types of chorus allow the individual who is having difficulty to practise in a less exposed situation. So a judicious mixture of chorus and individual repetition is needed, but with the emphasis on the various types of chorus[11], since only here do all or most have a chance to try out the new language.

A tiny step away from repetition on the road to autonomy is quasi-repetition: the teacher asks a question which already contains the answer: *Elle part à midi?* — *Oui, elle part à midi.* The words are repeated, only the intonation has changed, but from the totally artificial exercise of complete repetition we have moved to an exchange that, however limited, is realistically possible.

The next little step along the road is what might be called the 'teacher-is-stupid' exchange:

Input: *Elle part à deux heures.*
Teacher: *Elle part à midi?*
Pupil (exasperated intonation encouraged): (*Mais*) *non, elle part à deux heures.*

This can be a valuable move away from straight repetition, especially if alternative negatives are encouraged (*non; mais non; ah non; non, non*) with appropriate intonation, and if the teacher occasionally throws in a correct question (*Elle part à deux heures?*) so that *oui/non* (plus subsequent sentence intonation) also has to be manipulated. Further along this road are the gradually more difficult teacher questions designed to bring repetition of the input:

59

— *Elle part à deux heures ou à midi?*
— *Elle part à minuit, à midi ou à deux heures?*
— *Quand est-ce qu'elle part?*
— *Qui part à deux heures?*
— *Que fait Yvette cet après-midi?* etc.

After repetition comes the first stage of manipulation of the input. The sort of questioning outlined above will have alerted the learner to the manipulative possibilities of the input in so far as he has *heard* some of them used, though he has himself only been asked to reproduce the input. Now we want him to produce *Elle part à midi/deux heures/minuit et demi* etc., *Elle/Pierre/je/tu par(t)(s) à midi, Ils/les garçons/elles partent à midi, Nous partons/vous partez à midi,* or whatever. We may indeed be quite uninterested in the paradigm and want to make sure *part à* sticks; or we may want to ensure *elle part à* is followed by accurate times, or we may want to extend the verb slot, perhaps as *elle part/arrive/s'arrête/repart à*. The direction in which we actually extend and practise material depends very much on how we have planned the third stage, how we see our pupils actually using their new language material. The practise-all-the-paradigm approach at this stage often betokens a lack of thought-out connection in this last respect: its objective is a grammatical one ('Can't leave it till they know all the parts') rather than an instrumental one ('How are they going to use this next?'). In fact the two may sometimes coincide, as they do with the present of *partir*. But this is by no means always the case: try to find likely real life uses for all the parts of the future of *connaître*, for instance!

This form of extension of learned input is of course pattern drilling. It is important, if we accept research findings and general experience in rejecting the language laboratory as a teaching tool in the beginners course we are considering[12], that we should not throw out the baby with the bathwater and reject the pattern drill. It needs to be seen not as an end in itself but as a step along the way to a clear objective in stage three, and it needs in itself to be realistic. Students, even those as young as 11, will accept the need for abstract practice on the way to a useful end, if the relationship between practice and the end is clear and if the practice does not go on too long. However, as with presentation, to make the practice interesting in itself has the additional advantage of strengthening motivation, of making this stage of the process much less of a burden. For instance:

Ring your friend and find out what she's wearing to go out this afternoon.

Pattern: — *Tu portes ton pantalon bleu?*
ta chemise jaune?
. . . . . .
Non, je ne porte pas mon/ma . . . . . .
Oui, je porte mon/ma . . . .

With pairwork based on this after revision of clothes and colours, *ne* . . . *pas* and *ton/ta→mon/ma* are practised in a realistic mini-situation that can lead on to more open-ended dialogue on colours and clothes at stage three. The motivational power of this is far greater than that of a mechanical pattern exercise that says 'Put the following sentences into the negative: *Je porte mon pantalon bleu. Tu portes ta chemise jaune* . . .' whilst achieving the same objective. A good, modern textbook will do this for you: if not, inventiveness, and maybe some visuals, are called for. Even if the book offers all you need in this line, the occasional activity or exercise produced specially by the teacher for her own pupils, as with presentation materials, does wonders in personalizing learning.

The third stage is that of autonomous use. Far too many teachers, alas, never reach this third stage. They follow up what may be very competent teaching of presentation and reproduction stages by a few written exercises and go on to the next piece of input. Why should this be? In part, as with so many other things, it is a hangover from Grammar-Translation method. The *prose* was the point, the culmination of each unit. Language input, grammar input, testing exercises, all led to the prose translation. The most popular textbooks of the thirties and forties followed the same sequence, even if, as a bow to Direct Method, exercise instructions were incongruously and often incomprehensibly given in the foreign language.[13] The prose was the written high spot of each section, and if there is now no prose, well, a written exercise of whatever kind will have to do as a substitute. It is extremely difficult for a teacher brought up in a different tradition to *really* accept that the point, the end, the objective of each unit should be speech uncontrolled by her. Both noun and participle offend. They also, for the pupils, make modern languages a rather odd subject. Perhaps only in English is the expression of personal opinions orally a major objective, and there it is only one of very many.

Part of the problem, too, is that the teacher may have to fall back much more on her own resources in devising material for this aspect of her work. Older textbooks simply ignore it; more modern ones that try to set up classroom situations in which pupils actively *want* to express themselves in French, using the new material they have just practised as well as the old, run up against the difficulty of estimating just exactly what will turn on 2C in a particular school at a particular time. The teacher is in a better position: she can harness the world cup results, the exploits of the latest French pop star, or the fact that the Eiffel tower fell down yesterday, to give immediacy: the coursebook cannot. So suggested coursebook autonomous work needs to be supplemented much of the time by the teacher.

There are, however, two activities generating autonomous, communicative language which modern courses and modern classrooms can and do exploit, together or separately. These are pairwork and games. A personal illustration: the author discovered this combination for himself early in his secondary teaching career, having been told little about games and nothing about pairwork in his training. Oral revision of personal descriptions was planned for a bright fourth form, and the night before, after considerable brain-racking for something novel, the following idea arose. The class was to be paired. The 'A' members of each pair were given a piece of information to extract from the 'B' members (e.g. *le prénom de sa grand-mère*), who did not know what this was. The A members could ask any question they liked except the direct one, *Quel est le prénom de ta grand-mère?*; the aim of the B members of the pairs was to prevent the disclosure of the piece of information, whatever it might be, without ever refusing to answer a question (this wasn't allowed).

The game went very successfully, all the pieces of information related directly or indirectly to personal description, everybody practised appropriate if not totally accurate French and no one wanted to stop.

Analysing why the activity was successful afterwards pointed up the two elements: firstly pairwork, with sufficient background noise from other pairs for everyone to take a chance on their French knowing that only their partner would hear (and the teacher too when in earshot and specifically listening), so that there were few inhibitions in using their own French; secondly the fact that this was a game, with a partner who was an opponent and a clearly defined goal to achieve (or prevent your opponent from achieving), by appropriate cunning. Attention was almost totally removed from the medium (no one was sitting in silence thinking 'Is it an *être* or an *avoir* verb?') to the message ('Can I trick him into letting out her name by talking about his grandfather first?'). The result was uninhibited and (within the class's competence) fluent use of French, and material was produced that I was astonished to find they knew.

This road-to-Damascus example was with a high-ability fourth form: both activities — games and pairwork — need simplifying and modifying for use with first or second formers. But both are ways of producing a tolerably effective classroom substitute for, and of course preparation for, the use of French to get along in France. Something of this kind is vital to give continuing practice in the thought-less use of the French so far available to the student, if the first steps ashore in Calais or Paris are not to be the traumatic disappointment they were with the old Grammar-Translation method ('Five years French and an O level and I don't know how to get a cup of white coffee'). Let us look at each of these techniques in more detail.

The logic of pairwork is irrefutable. With a class of thirty-two, a thirty-two minute period devoted entirely to oral French would allow each pupil to spend thirty seconds speaking in conversation with the teacher, fifteen and a half minutes listening to his fellows, and sixteen minutes listening to the teacher. And that in an ideal and totally unrealistic situation without pauses, use of English, need for correction or disciplining, and with the whole period devoted to the one activity. There is no way that effective oral production can be learned like this. The substitution of the one-to-one relationship of the language laboratory in theory overcame this: in practice the limitations imposed by programming and the dehumanizing effect of 'talking to' a machine led to boredom and lack of learning. Paired work gives the comparative efficiency (sixteen minutes active speaking in the model situation outlined above[14]) without the repetitious straight-jacket of the programmed tape and with a real interlocutor to interact with. Clearly it is not without its snags, and these should not be minimized. Firstly, noise. In point of fact, pairwork produces no more noise and disturbance to the class next door tha well-organized chorus work, and a good deal less than that sometimes produced by music or metalwork. As in these lessons, the noise is a productive noise. Secondly, discipline. This is more a problem in anticipation than fact. Student teachers trying out pairwork for the first time come back to their tutor glowing: 'It worked, they all did it, they were all using French!' Of course it will not work any better than regular classwork in discipline terms. If the classwork is unruly, pairwork will be too. But if classwork is well organized and the discipline good because the pupils have been led to want to learn, there will be no additional trouble with pairwork. Thirdly, it is suggested, pairwork reinforces error. There is some truth in this, though a pair in disagreement about how to express something can always put up a hand and ask the teacher: it is certainly essential for the teacher to be on hand and alert to this. Still, there will indeed be *some* reinforcement of error, just as there is when we allow pupils to go to France and waiters and ticket-sellers and other busy Frenchmen don't correct their French. The point is to prepare the pairwork thoroughly with the class as a whole before allowing individual pairs to begin, then to accept that *at this stage in the learning process*, though not at other points, there will be some degree of error accepted as a trade-off against the value of the practice in fluency. Better to be able to say a great deal with some mistakes than nearly nothing with elegant accuracy. The final point raised against pairwork is that, especially in the early stages of learning a language, on the sort of course we are currently dealing with, learners have little or nothing of their own that they can say. Let us look at this point in some detail, for it leads us into a consideration of the organization and use of pairwork.

We have already seen that the three stages of teaching new material overlap, and that controlled pattern-practice exercises can be placed in an imaginary situation and practised in pairs. Pairwork cannot be expected to take pupils much further than this along the road to true autonomy in the earliest stages, but gradually the areas in which the individual takes control can be expanded. A pairwork exercise at this early level relating to the function of 'expressing ownership' might consist of the pair assembling as many personal classroom objects as they can whose French names are known (*un livre, un stylo, un stylo à bille, un crayon, un classeur* . . .), mixing them and then sorting out their ownership, pretending to be strangers. The work, first demonstrated in front of the class, then prepared by chorus repetition of the basic structure, would be based on:

— *Tiens, j'ai trouvé un* . . . . . . *C'est votre* . . . . . ., *monsieur?*
— *Oui merci, vous avez trouvé mon* . . . . . .
— *Ah non, ce n'est pas mon* . . . . . .

Limited variations are possible, but basically this is practising *votre/mon*. With a change of roles the whole exercise will last only four minutes.[15] By the end of our two-year course, pairwork which may well look more like the following should be possible, based on cut-outs of clothing items handed to the pairs, or an overhead projector drawing of a great array of clothes.

A: *Votre ami(e) arrive chez vous pour passer le week-end, mais il/elle a laissé sa valise chez lui/elle.*

> *Vous lui proposez qu'il/elle emprunte quelques-uns de vos propres vêtements.*
>
> **B:** *Vous trouvez ça gentil, mais . . . vous n'aimez pas tous les vêtements qu'il/elle propose!*
> *Vous acceptez les uns, vous rejetez les autres — mais toujours avec tact!*

Here two pupils, chosen for their relative fluency, are first manipulated more or less as puppets by the teacher to build up the scene with class suggestions as to what might be said next. Then pairs are allowed to re-enact their own versions. By this point in the course the only thing really determined by the teacher is the area (clothing) in which the exchange is to take place, plus expressions of pleasure and tactful rejection. In practice much is taken from the instructions (this is the point of using French here, where English at first sight looks much easier). Scenes in 'French' like this emerge:

— *Ah Jeanne, j'ai laissé ma valise chez moi.*
— *Non!*
— *Si!*
— *Veux-tu mes vêtements?*
— *Ah, où sont tes vêtements?*
— *Voilà. Dans l'armoire. Aimes-tu cette robe?*
— *Oui, elle est jolie, mais je n'aime pas bleu.*
— *Préfères-tu cette jupe?*
— *Oui, elle est très jolie, mais je n'aime pas les jupes.*
— *Aimes-tu ce pantalon?*
— *C'est très gentil, Jeanne, mais le pantalon est trop gros . . .*

and so on.

The French will leave something to be desired, but the level of accuracy is sufficient for clear communication. It gives the pupils opportunities for practice, using their own French for a purpose they are prepared to make their own. This last point is important. Working privately with a friend in pairwork, the imaginary situation superimposed, the visual materials added — all these make it easier to accept the teacher's request for suspension of disbelief and for involvement in a near-realistic use of French. What is so vital is this personal involvement, this readiness to accept for a moment their own and their partner's version of French as the medium of communication, to feel that they really have something to say and can actually find the means to say it. The addition of the games element to pairwork helps to remove another layer of artificiality and intensify the drive to communicate.

There is nothing new in classroom games.[16] Generations of

student-teachers of modern languages have been encouraged to adapt simple games in order to practise particular language points and have found tremendous enthusiasm from pupils. The only snags are that on the one hand the linguistic point may get lost in the enthusiasm for the game, with discipline also suffering, and on the other that too few people may get a chance to use their foreign language in the course of the game. Versions of bingo, for instance, may suffer horrendously from both faults. But properly organized games can set up in class an atmosphere in which pupils genuinely feel impelled from within to use their French.

The combination of this with pairwork, which gives everyone an opportunity to use their French at the same time, leads to one of the most productive forms of autonomous language use. 'First-to-finish' games are easy: here is a simple example based on Relationships.

> 'A' pupils are given a character (*Tu es Eustache Dumoulin et tu as 91 ans*) and a family tree on a banda sheet, which they must conceal from their partner. 'B' pupils must try to reconstruct the family tree on a sheet of paper by asking questions of A, Eustache Dumoulin. The first pair in which B manages this wins.

There are some organizational problems with pair games. Pairs can overhear other pairs and derive information from them (this makes the game less fair, but *linguistically* it's fine, of course); the temptation for B to cheat by looking at A's sheet or by using English is greater when there is a winning-post to reach. With some classes the patrolling presence of the teacher may be enough; with others the issue of penalty points may be necessary. But this sort of organizational problem is not difficult to overcome: with most classes the liking for the activity is such that considerable goodwill is brought to it.[17]

Let us recapitulate. So far we have considered the three basic stages of presentation, reproduction, and autonomous use in relation to aural comprehension and oral production. What of the other skills of reading and writing? And what of the civilization content of the course?

Reading as a skill has been rather neglected in the last thirty years. It was not just that the pure audio-visual and audio-lingual courses were spoken-word oriented: the learning theories underpinning them demanded controlled intensive work rather than extensive exposure to the language in any form. Before them, too, there was only a limited tradition of reading experience in the foreign language in the Grammar-Translation method or the interwar compromise methods. 'Readers' were treated as extended unseen translation, to be read aloud paragraph by paragraph by the pupils and then translated slowly and laboriously. There is little evidence of pupils being taught to read silently or given an opportunity to do this with appropriate-level materials in language teaching programmes. Kelly[18] suggests that extensive reading, aimed at rapid assimilation of ideas rather than analysis of grammatical structure, and definitely distinguished from translation, has only in this century been recognized as a skill in its own right as opposed to intensive reading. The distinction as a basis for silent reading as a specific skill appears to have been first made by Palmer: 'Reading may be extensive or intensive. In the first, each sentence is subjected to a careful scrutiny — in the latter book after book will be read through without giving more than a superficial and passing attention to the lexicological units of which it is composed.'[19]

The pupils on our self-contained language-experience course are hardly likely to reach the stage of reading book after book, either during or at the end of the course. Intensive reading may be important, however, indeed vital. At the simplest level reading 'SIGNORI' and 'SIGNORE' for gist may produce distinct embarrassment in Italy — 'careful scrutiny' of the notices outside the Italian lavatories is needed. It is just this sort of notice language (Does that sign mean 'bus lane' or 'bus stop'? What exactly do these instructions on the tin mean?) that is of most practical use for basic comprehension in the foreign language. It presents problems in that the register used in some languages may be very different from that of the spoken language (this is particularly true of German, where convoluted language is at a premium in official public notices). But a limited range of basic notice language seems necessary in view of the aims of the sort of course we have in mind, and it is, incidentally, popular with pupils because of its obvious application, especially when taught from photographs.[20]

But skills are not separate, and reading, extensive reading, that is, quite apart from its use in its own right, has a positive effect on the other skills, especially aural comprehension. Her Majesty's Inspectors have for some years been concerned with the lack of attention to extensive reading: in *Modern Languages in the Comprehensive School* they bemoaned the fact that in many schools they visited even the most able pupils were simply 'not taught the invaluable skill of rapid silent reading'. The difficulty is that silent reading takes time to develop and has to be programmed regularly into the timetable; in addition it presupposes that the pupil already possesses a fair amount of available spoken and heard language in the appropriate register. The register problem can be overcome by using readers that are, initially, largely in dialogue, corresponding to the sort of language that has been heard and learned in spoken-language lessons. It seems none the less reasonable to assume that in practical terms the introduction of extensive reading cannot really take place until some time in the second year and that the most that can reasonably be expected, as a basic objective, is that the pupil will have read five or six short readers (really short: the highly simplified, heavily illustrated type, about sixteen pages long, of which there are many on the market) silently for gist by the end of the two-year course.[21]

How should such reading be developed? Silent reading is not so much taught as learned. The two most important factors are practice and the removal of stumbling blocks. Practice means devoting the equivalent of at least one period per fortnight to it, once the stage has been reached where it can reasonably begin. It also means having materials that are not too difficult (readers meant for class reading aloud are far too difficult for individual silent reading) and having a variety of readers that will interest different pupils, but all of them lively, up-to-date, and attractively presented.

What of the stumbling blocks? The three greatest are: reading your first reader; reading the first page of any reader; and having ready access to vocabulary. The first problem can be tackled by adding the crutch of oral reading by the teacher: all the class have the same reader and follow the teacher's reading in their books. When comprehension work shows that the gist of the reader has been generally absorbed with the class using the double intake from ear and eye, the second stage can be moved to, in which the class all still have copies of the same reader, but only the first page is read by the teacher with the class following in their books: the rest of the reader is then read silently. The first page is a stumbling block because in any short narrative this represents the bulk of the story-setting and character establishment: the reader has to adjust to the author's style and at the same time the first page usually has the greatest concentration of new and specialist words. Once over this 'establishing' page, comprehension becomes easier in terms both of language and narrative. When comprehension questions reveal that pupils can produce gist comprehension after silent reading of all but the first page, the first-page crutch is also removed and pupils can read the next readers silently on their own. From now on it is no longer necessary for all pupils to be reading the same book at the same time: a private question-and-answer session with the teacher when they bring up a book to exchange it provides the teacher with feedback on the comprehension taking place. The third stumbling block, vocabulary, means that the teacher needs to be always available as a walking dictionary. The usual problem sequence ('I can't get that sentence' — hand up — 'That sentence there, Miss' — translation from teacher) then proceeds as rapidly as possible and the pupil, his concentration on the message of the text disturbed as little as possible, returns to his gist-reading of French as rapidly as possible. What we are aiming for here, in the reading skill, is exactly the same as in the oral skills: it is pupil autonomy. It is the use of his own, here, print-decoding abilities to take in a message *that he wants to know about*, just as in oral autonomous work he was, we hope, putting out a message he wanted to express. Reading in this sense is an entirely different skill from reading aloud, for which there should be a very limited place in a language-experience course.[22] Reading aloud is also a difficult skill to acquire, with almost no direct application.

What then of writing? In view of the position generally taken *vis-à-vis* writing, that it is the least valuable of the four skills in its own right, there may well be a lot of bad consciences around, as we suggested in Chapter 1, about the amount of time that pupils devote to it. Certainly at the level we are considering in this chapter any writing done will have to be justified in terms of its indirect results, whether as reinforcement or as relief.

The relief arguments are the weakest. 'Neither they nor I could get through a double period without it' is slightly suspect. Aural comprehension, oral production, face-to-face exchange of language, silent reading: have all the possible imaginative variants of these been tried, to lend variety and hold interest and attention? And in particular has the civilization of the country whose language we are teaching been sufficiently explored? There is a wealth of work possible here, extremely valuable in terms of the ends we have outlined for the language-experience course and at the same time quite different in classroom terms from the language work. It is one of a number of ways in which the putting of pen to paper may occur in a language lesson (true/false comprehension exercises are another) without the use of any extensive written forms of the foreign language. And especially in a mixed-ability group at this level, the attempt to teach written French as a skill must be a dubious and unrewarding pastime for both teacher and taught.

But if the 'necessary relief' arguments are weak and smack of unimaginative teaching, the 'reinforcement' arguments are stronger. If we look at the sort of exercise used at this language-experience level, both by examination of textbooks and by observation of teachers' own materials, we find that it is to a very large extent copy-writing, often cleverly disguised, to reinforce material already learned aurally or orally. Typical exercises from such courses as *Éclair, A Paname, Entente cordiale, Hexagone*[23] involve copying the correct word from a printed selection into a gap in a printed sentence, copying out a whole sentence with a filled gap, reorganizing printed words (or sentences) into sensible sentences (or paragraphs), completing sentences with endings that have been seen elsewhere, answering questions that contain the answer, working out anagrams of short, known words, and the like. This is in addition to other 'written' work — colouring, ticking true/false, choosing alternatives in multiple-choice questions, drawing to foreign language instructions, underlining error or divergence — which, though involving a pen, can in no way be seen as promoting the skill of writing in the foreign language. Even the more traditional audio-visual courses, such as the second version of *Longman Audio-Visual French*, rely to a large extent on the production of a sequence of sentences using orally practised material and differing in only one element from a given model: a written slot-substitution exercise, in fact. This is near copy-writing for reinforcement.

A teacher using such exercises may quite reasonably justify them simply as an additional reinforcement, maybe set as homework, of language learned primarily for oral and aural use. But she does need to beware! It takes most children of eleven an unconscionably long time to get even a short copying exercise down on paper. What is theoretically reinforcement may easily be taking half of a thirty-five minute period. This sort of half oral, half written lesson may quickly become the norm. With the extremely limited amount of time at our disposal this seems an incompetent way of proceeding, an inefficient means to the ends we have set. Easily the lesson degenerates into what the Americans tellingly call 'busy work'. Some writing for reinforcement seems justified, but a close watch on how much is used and how justifiable it really is needs to be kept vigilantly.

Time spent on civilization can certainly be justified, though, in relation to our aims. At this level we need to make our entrée into French civilization at a real place with real people. Ideally, and more and more frequently in reality, too, this can be the place that it is proposed to visit at the end of the course. Even if such a visit is not possible, a link-up via local town twinning, school-exchange school, staff personal contact, or the assistant's home is always possible. The link can be made more real through photos (preferably linked directly with audio material and realia), *correspondance sonore* on cassette, written and printed material, and small portable realia. Much knowledge and insight can then proceed not from abstract questions like 'What do the French eat?' but from direct interrogation on tape of a French partner: 'Listen, Pierre, this is what I had for my meals yesterday — what did you have? And another thing, in the last tape I didn't understand what you meant by *ficelle* . . .' Instead of the abstract generalization 'What is a typical French town like?' we have the personal and precise: 'But what is Rouen like? What do *you* do in the evening there, where do *you* go shopping, how do *you* travel about?' With this sort of personalization — individual members of the English class speaking to individual members of the French class — and with material produced in the mother tongue but comprehended in the foreign language (the reverse is either too difficult or too trivial for civilization purposes), such a *correspondance sonore*, efficiently run, can be the medium for attaining all the civilization aims of the language-experience course that we have laid out. Better still, of course, that such a correspondence should be merely the preliminary to an actual visit to actual people. The course can be planned to fan out from the individual (what do you do, what do you wear, what do you eat, what do you drink . . .?) to the home, then the town, then the region. The teacher's role (and the assistant's, for she too can be effectively used for this) is to form the necessary generalization, to show where what Jean-Pierre says is generalizable to French boys only, or to people of his age, or to people in his area, or to the French generally. From this comes the contrast not just between Kevin and Jean-Pierre, but between Jean-Pierre and other Frenchmen. As the time for the visit approaches, the questions and answers of the *correspondance sonore* should be more and more specifically geared to it, so that the English pupils arrive in France with clear expectations which will be by and large fulfilled, and with the unexpected and unexplained at the periphery rather than at the centre of their experience.

The visit, then, is really an essential part of the course. An exchange visit is hardly possible for a course of this kind where all second-form pupils are involved and in large schools a week's visit for all, however organized, may be impossible during a single week of term. The visit may have to be shorter than a week and there may have to be two or even three visits organized in separate weeks.

Timetable disruptions are always a problem with language visits, but if the visit is kept to the end of the course, as it should be, being the culmination of it, the period involved at the end of the summer term is one when other subject teachers are prepared to release pupils with less fuss than at other times of year. Whether the visit is based on an LEA-owned centre, a town-twinning arrangement, arrangements with a pre-existing exchange school or even commercially booked *pension* accommodation, it must be carefully organized to allow the pupils to demonstrate *to themselves* that they can function at a certain level in the situations they have practised when faced with them in reality. The way that this is done will depend on what has gone before: if there has been a build-up by *correspondance sonore*, with each pupil twinned with a French pupil, and if the visit can take place under the wing of the corresponding school, the work can be based on face-to-face exchanges between the French-English pairs. There may, alternatively, be other readily-available French people prepared to function as informants and interlocutors. Contacts may perhaps have to be made from scratch. In any event each pupil needs something like a diary with set situations, perhaps arranged on set days, and questions and tasks, arising from these situations, to accomplish. The results of accomplishing these tasks, the information gained, can then be written up at the end of each day.[24] The situations and tasks must of course be based directly on the practice situations worked on through the course: the two must interlock. Ideally the visit would be planned first in detail and coursework geared to this end. In practice it may only be possible to plan in general terms, but topics such as the ones detailed on pages 50–52 should not be difficult to prepare for precisely.

This then is the sort of course we may effectively present to the pupils as self-contained and useful with a specific end in view, opening their eyes to a different culture and giving them something of the language of that culture that will be of direct value in reaching that end. They should be returning from the visit feeling that something has been achieved and with the belief that mastery of the language could in fact now be built on what they *have* achieved. For more pupils than is otherwise the case there will also be the motivation to attempt that mastery.

Should such a course be examined? In a sense, the visit *is* the examination, in that it is a self-examination. Just as the end-product from each 'chunk' of input on the course should be autonomous comprehension and use of language, and successful learning of the input is demonstrated by the ability at this third stage to use it as their own language, so for the course as a whole the visit represents the genuine point of autonomous use and the pupil makes his own decision as to what he has achieved. His decision on whether to continue with a foreign language will be partly a product (indeed, often largely a product) of this success or lack of success. So it may be counter-productive to incorporate also an end-of-course test (the temptation is to use a Graded Test); however, if such a test *is* incorporated it needs to be devised in a sophisticated way to include the visit within the central area of testing.[25] If relative success or failure depends not on the true end-product, the visit, but on a separate examination, we have moved our language teaching back a step from the practice-for-reality objective to the old practice-for-practice's-sake. We are back in the old bind that leads to pupils' rejection of language learning altogether.

The pupil who does decide to continue with his foreign language learning beyond this self-contained two-year course will find that things are from now on somewhat different: he will be embarking on a new course that has much longer-term and differently organized objectives. However, the approach and methods should again be genuinely geared to those objectives so that the positive view of language learning generated by the language-experience course will not be dissipated. We shall consider the implications of teaching language for mastery in the next chapter.

Footnotes

[1] Here is an obvious area where the range of comprehension is large (waiters are not particularly limited in their question forms in most languages); so in a mixed-ability group, though all would be expected to respond to the waiter, the least able are going to have to deploy *Comment Monsieur?* and *Monsieur, je ne comprends pas* until they get, one hopes, a simple enough version. The brightest will have a range of question-types they understand.

[2] The clash here between what the teacher thinks is useful restaurant language (remembering that gorgeous Frenchman who took her to Lapérouse) and what the pupils think is (probably MacDonald's basic list) must be resolved in favour of the pupils if the *end* of the course is their visit to France.

[3] Much of this is unnecessary if the TV is in the hotel room; however, at the sort of level we are dealing with the pupil is much more likely to encounter it in a hotel lobby or lounge, or in a private house or hostel.

[4] Some people would, and do, go much further, building a whole language-awareness course into the first year of foreign language teaching, often before any foreign language is taught, with a history of language development, non-verbal communication, language relationships, simple linguistic concepts, and so on. Unfortunately a good deal of this has to remain inert at this age, dealing

as it does with languages and concepts of which the pupil has no direct experience. On the whole it seems better to allow these comparative ideas to arise from the perceived difference between the language the pupil knows and the one he is learning. Develop them then by all means, but let the linguistics be an explanation of problems arising rather than an abstract structure.

⁵ At times it can be funny. The author's eleven-year-old daughter, in her first year of French, arriving on a family holiday at an overnight stop at Maintenon, asked, puzzled: 'Does this town-name mean something, Daddy? Our French teacher's always saying that at the beginning of sentences.'

⁶ And, of course, they use it constantly as such outside their French classes in other parts of their learning. For research evidence on the importance of the printed word as such in language learning see Lambert W. E. 'Psychological approaches to the study of language. Part I: On learning, thinking and human abilities' *Modern Language Journal* 47, (1963); Mueller T. and Leutenegger R. 'Some inferences about an intensified oral approach to the teaching of French based on a study of course drop-outs' *Modern Language Journal* 48 (1964); and Dodson C. J. and Price J. E. 'The role of the printed word in foreign-language learning' *Modern Languages* XLVII (1966).

⁷ Burstall C. (op. cit.) p. 168.

⁸ And Moskowitz, for instance, found considerable dislike among primary-age schoolchildren of their passive role where television was used as a medium of instruction (not just presentation). See Moskowitz G. 'TV versus classroom instruction in foreign languages' *Journal of Experimental Education* 33 (1964). The question of interaction with the *computer* screen we will deal with in Chapter 8: presentation of new material to a full class via computers, with the possibility of individual pupil interaction with the programme, is hardly feasible at the moment.

⁹ Comenius J. A. *Orbis Sensualium Pictus* (op. cit.). Preface.

¹⁰ Research evidence constantly shows a relationship between amount of foreign language used in the classroom and effectiveness of learning. Burstall (op. cit.) found this at primary level; Carroll found it at university level (Carroll J. B. *The Foreign Language Attainments of Language Majors in the Senior Year* Harvard University 1967) and again in his major comparative international survey of factors producing success in foreign-language learning at the secondary level (Carroll J. B. *The Teaching of French as a Foreign Language in Eight Countries* Wiley 1975): 'Students placed in a teaching situation where they use French in the classroom a substantial amount of the time, and rarely the mother tongue, have a decided advantage over students in classrooms where the opposite situation prevails.' (Carroll 1975 p. 34.)

¹¹ It is salutary to have a colleague, or the assistant, sit in on a lesson and, pinpointing a single pupil, write down all that the pupil says in the lesson. What sounds from the front like intensive and varied oral repetition work with ready, loud, accurate responses from the class as a whole looks very different from the individual learner's viewpoint. Much of that section of the lesson will have been spent listening in silence: or, of course, with children with a short attention span, not listening, in noise!

¹² See chapter 2, footnote 18.

¹³ See, for example, Collins H. F. *A French Course for Schools* Macmillan 1930, perhaps the most popular French textbook of the period.

¹⁴ Not of course in practice; though even in practice something like the 32:1 ratio in favour of pairwork holds good.

¹⁵ Pairwork, where each pupils simply turns to his or her neighbour, is so

much more practical in classroom terms than groupwork for these short but valuable bursts.

[16] M. Buckby and D. F. Grant's useful compendium, *Faites vos jeux* (Nuffield Foundation) has been around since 1971.

[17] For further ideas for expanding the autonomous-use stage of language learning, see Chapter 4 of Littlewood, W. *Communicative Language Teaching* Cambridge University Press 1981.

[18] Kelly L. G. (op. cit.) p. 150.

[19] Palmer H. E. *The Scientific Study and Teaching of Languages* London 1917, p. 204.

[20] Modern courses include practice in this sort of comprehension. Alternatively there are Harrap's useful series *French Sign Language* (Pearce M. R. and Ellis D. L. 1975), *German Sign Language* (Sawyers R. 1975), etc.

[21] The Oxford University Press Rapid-Reading French series, first published in 1931 (Gurney D. and Scott G. C. eds.) and still in print in the 1960s, was an early attempt to develop extensive reading via carefully limited French. The editors themselves were well aware of the fact that 'the usual treatment of the Text in language-teaching tends to concentration on form' and that 'if intensive reading is varied by no other reading exercise the pupil will be apt to forget the real purpose of his reading, which is to grasp the content of the passage as a whole' (quotations from the 1931 Foreword to the series). However, they refused to prescribe a method ('The stories can of course be used in any way which will, in the teacher's judgement, train the pupils to read') and in very many schools the 'rapid' readers were used for the traditional plodding task of reading aloud and translating.

[22] Burstall (op. cit.) again, found that, questioning pupils after two years in the secondary school, 'One aspect of learning French in the secondary school which appeared to be universally disliked was the practice of reading aloud in French'. Burstall quotes pupils' comments, including the revealing: 'French is hard to read and understand, because it is not spelt like it sounds. I cannot understand what I am reading out aloud, but I can understand when someone talks to me.'

[23] Henry J. and Lockeyear J. (eds.) *Éclair* ILEA 1975; Lillo M. and Sprake D. *A Paname* E. J. Arnold 1977; Naylor J. A. and Bird E. *Entente cordiale* Hodder and Stoughton 1979; Foden K. *Hexagone* O.U.P. 1983.

[24] The Longman series of workbooks 'Go to Calais', 'Go to Boulogne' etc. are useful in offering a starting point for this sort of thing, but the material for such a week's visit needs to be extended and personalized more. Planning the diary and the tasks to be performed may well involve a preliminary visit by a member of staff.

[25] We shall be looking at such test possibilities in greater detail in Chapter 9.

5   The specialist course to age 16

The third secondary school year, in the form of organization we have proposed, is the first of a three-year, self-contained course whose recipients are largely self-selected. Within the curricular organization of most secondary schools this is the best arrangement that can be hoped for. It may be, however, that the language-specialism option is not available until the fourth year: this is quite frequently the case. Then the specialist course will have to be crushed into two years and the language-experience course expanded to three. In fact there are some areas that can be transferred in this case from the specialist to the general course: extensive reading for all can easily be further developed during the additional third year, additional work on aural comprehension of topic-related dialogues can also be viewed as useful for both those who will continue and those who will complete[1], and the introduction here in year three of narrative aural comprehension can be justified in the short as well as the long run. It is strange how aural comprehension and oral production of narrative are often seen as unreal in comparison with stichomythic dialogue, alternating line for line and person to person. They are certainly more difficult, but not less directly useful. Listen to the conversation in the Sunday-morning saloon bar of the average pub. It consists of A narrating, with B, C, and D listening, with the occasional encouraging interjection to jolly A along and get him to the end of his story as quickly as possible so that B, C, and D, with the absolutely minimal bridge-phrase ('Very interesting that, just the same sort of thing happened to me . . .'), can each have their turn to narrate. This saloon-bar mode is a very common one in general conversation, for which classroom practice initially of aural comprehension of narrative, and then of the more difficult oral production of narrative, is necessary preparation.

Returning to our third year: if this has to be a compromise, it is important that work done at this stage should be seen as relevant by both types of pupil, and particularly that, if groups at this level are setted by ability, varying programmes should not prevent some pupils making the language choice at the end of the third year. With a two-year language-experience course it is easy to avoid 'sink' groups; with three years there is a temptation, too often succumbed to, to separate the O-level and CSE groups and send them ahead, leaving the rest — often 60% of the pupils — to work through the year, seeing themselves inevitably as language failures. To do this invalidates the whole point of the language-experience course, which is to give something that is both complete in itself and a possible base for further language study for anyone. If we face this fact honestly, the linear-grammar based course will have to be held back until the fourth year, when the specialist course begins, if we are not to present something truncated to those who will not continue beyond the third year.

So whether we are to have two or three years for it, our mastery course will be different, more intensive, but must be based on the foundations of the experience course. Let us assume for the moment that the specialist course is in the same language (almost always French) as that of the initial years. If languages are changed, and of course where a second language is added, the problems are greater: we shall return to them.

The temptation with the specialist course is to revert to something not far from Grammar-Translation. The feeling that two, three years even have been spent on aural-oral language and civilization and that now it's time for something serious is strong. 'Something serious' equals grammar, written grammatical exercises, written composition and, as soon as possible, back-papers from the looming examination. This temptation is particularly strong with a separate O-level group, but it is still there even with pupils who will take CSE and 16+. Realistically, passing the examination must form part of one's aims, but this must not become one's sole aim. It is, I would suggest, largely compatible with the general educational aims of a specialist course to age 16 as outlined in chapter 3. In a moment we shall consider the balance of skills at this level and appropriate techniques to promote them, but first let us look at the place of grammar, because at this point it takes on a somewhat different role.

Grammar so far, in the language-experience course, has been explanatory, comparative in a limited sort of way, inevitably unstructured, largely peripheral. Now we need to cover all the useful basic grammar, systematically and rapidly. Taking French as an example: we need to institute a programme that organizes and clarifies for the pupil the formation of the present tense of the regular verb and other common present tense verb patterns, question formulation, negatives, partitives, possessives, demonstratives, adjective position and agreement, the regular perfect with *avoir*, the *aller* future, imperative forms, direct object pronouns and maybe the present of reflexive verbs. These can all be covered fairly rapidly, since from the point of view of grammar this will be revision plus expansion, but they now need to form a coherently interrelating structure, progressively built up. Clearly this should not be done as grammar teaching *in vacuo* but must be based on 'texts' in the widest sense of the word: spoken dialogue, spoken narrative, some printed dialogue and narrative. A judicious use of 'double input' (text heard and seen at the same time) will help with new materials or modes (e.g. in the early stages of moving from dialogue to narrative), but in general we should now be presenting only aurally materials that are aimed at aural comprehension, and only in printed form those that are aimed at comprehension of the printed word.

There may well be a problem of suitable commercial materials here. There are currently not many courses on the market that allow such a rapid organization or re-organization of French at third or fourth-form level with appropriate materials and that aim to complement and follow-up a language-experience course such as *Éclair* or *Action*.[2] It may well be, for instance, that if, say, Longman B3 is to be tackled half-way through the first year of the specialist course, that the languages department and/or the individual teacher will have to produce their own special materials for this first half year, in the form of taped dialogues and passages, banda worksheets, pairwork exercises, appropriate visual materials and a simple banda grammar based on this material and covering the sort of grammar topics listed above.[3] This sort of approach is not quite so second-best as it sounds. Good materials for half a year's work are by no means impossible for a well-run department to produce collectively, and such a course can then be an accurately designed bridge from a specific commercial course of one kind to a specific commercial course of another. The materials can be made appropriate to the knowledge and interests of the particular pupils in that school and will have the additional motivational advantage that, at the beginning of this new specialist course, materials personally designed for the pupils are being presented to them.

The list of grammar topics above has some elements which would be common to all languages at this stage (present tense of regular verbs, question forms, negatives, and so on), some which might be left until later in other languages because of greater complexity, and some omissions in French which in other languages would need to be included. There are some areas, such as the early introduction of the regular form of the perfect, and the *aller* future, which are extremely useful and made possible by the fact that these will undoubtedly have been met already in some of their parts in the language-experience course.

There need not, in such a course, be a violent shift from situation work: the grammatical point presented can be embedded in a situation that includes elements already known from the language-experience course, but regrouped or extended to hold the interest. So the perfect of verbs in *-u* plus clothing may produce, say, a sequence of scenes at the lost-property office which can now develop and extend clothing and colour adjective vocabulary further than when they were met in the language-experience course in a different situation, whilst introducing a grammatical extension of the perfect of verbs in *-é* already covered.

What of the skills to be developed in this tailor-made bridge course?

Aural comprehension is undoubtedly important, and at this level we would put it first. Firstly because the hearing of and the deriving of clear messages from a great deal of spoken language is a necessary precursor to attempting to use one's own French in face-to-face exchanges at a more sophisticated level. Knowing what your interlocutor has said is a necessary preliminary to responding to it by answering, contradicting, obeying, extending, or changing the subject. Familiarity with intonation patterns, sentence forms, fillers (be honest, weren't you thrown the first time a Frenchman said *'bon ben'* to you?), regional accent variety of a general kind (e.g. *midi* versus north) helps remove the problems of the medium and allows the learner to concentrate on the message. But equally a largely understood message enables him to abstract new material from the heard French and, however gingerly, try it out as his own. It may be part of the message itself:

— *Un congélateur? Alors, c'est une sorte de réfrigérateur.*
— *Ah oui, bien sûr . . . oui, nous, nous avons un . . . congélateur.*

or it may be picked consciously or unconsciously from the medium:

— He keeps starting an answer with *'Enfin . . .'* when he wants time to think. *I'll* try that next time.

or it may simply arise through repetition:

— *De l'argent en plus pour tous, c'est bien possible!*
— *C'est possible? Tu crois?*
— *Mais bien sûr!*

— *De l'argent en plus? Pour tous?*
— *Mais oui! Tu vas voir!*

This sort of extension of the spoken output as a result of the heard input arises all the time in real conversation; it is less direct where the aural input has no immediately following oral output (as is the case with most classroom aural comprehension work for most pupils), but none the less it still occurs. The equivalent 'real' situation is the increment in spoken French skills that undoubtedly occurs as a result of extensive listening to French radio or watching French TV or films.

Quite apart from its effect on spoken output, an increase in aural input is vital at this level to achieve the necessary imbalance between language-we-can-produce and language-we-can-understand.[4] The second is far greater in our mother tongue and also needs to be far greater in our second language. In the early stages of learning the foreign language (in our terms, during the language-experience course), though there will be an imbalance in favour of comprehension, it will be by no means large enough for our realistic needs in the longer term. We have all gone through that period in our language learning, surely, when we could say, however imperfectly, what we wanted, but were floored completely by what was said to us, where the answer to *Scusi, dov'è la via Garibaldi?* left us just as lost as when we started. This is the time, in the third and fourth year, the first two of our specialist course, to largely expand practice in aural recognition to the point where conversational comprehension, when the conversation is addressed to us and is on a familiar topic, really does take place.

Thirdly, aural comprehension aids written comprehension and vice versa once the two reach a certain level of attainment. *Je te l'ai déjà dit/emprunté/envoyé* etc., once it is a firmly recognized aural pattern with a clear meaning attached, is going to present that much less of a problem when met in the printed form, just as equivalent help to the spoken form can come from known printed forms. In the area of pronunciation and intonation competence especially, once a sentence read can trigger off at a silent level just below the threshold of speech a clearly formulated oral equivalent, there is reinforcement of aural comprehension by written comprehension.

One final pragmatic reason for stressing aural comprehension skills: many examinations at age 16 put a premium on comprehension, aural and written. Where this is the case, a pupil who is good at these hardly ever does really badly in the examination as a whole. This is not in itself a reason for stressing the comprehension skills at this level, but it is nice to feel that genuine language-learning objectives point for once in the same direction as the examination.

The skill of reading comprehension also needs to be developed. Our aim here is that by the end of the three-year course the best pupils should be able to tackle a simple modern French paperback, and that all pupils should be fluent enough in gist reading to read a magazine short story, a tourist brochure, or a popular newspaper article on a topic they know something about, and be confident that they can get the sense of it even though they are not clear about the meaning of every word. For this it is essential that the reader period every fortnight on a library basis be continued and also that pupils be encouraged to take their books home and continue to read them there. A homework may be formally devoted to this from time to time, but what should be encouraged is that the pupil reads the books for interest in the content and for the pleasantly rewarding feeling that his French is progressively improving, that he can read more and more easily: set too often as a formal homework, the reader can become a chore and a bore. Short, gradually more difficult readers still form the backbone of the work, but factual material also needs to be introduced ('Jean, the textbook's mentioned the Auvergne a couple of times this week — I've got this package of tourist stuff[5] about the Massif Central. Could you perhaps go through it and then tell us all in English for five minutes at the end of the lesson what you've found out about the Auvergne?'). The more that the language can be used as a tool the better, and from the fourth year on (the second of our specialist course) reading comprehension, if it has been systematically and thoroughly developed, can easily be used as such a tool. It can also be incorporated into more systematic civilization work, as we shall see.

If the two receptive areas have great importance at this level, it is equally important not to neglect oral production. The same three stages as were identified in Chapter 4 still apply here, of course, but it becomes progressively easier to organize the third, autonomous-use stage, especially if this is largely based on pairwork. Pupils should be encouraged to bring more and more of their own language variants into this, language constraints should gradually be relaxed, work should become progressively more open-ended. It is important that systematic revision and teaching of variants is done: everyone in this class can say *oui*, but do they know *d'accord, bien sûr, oui certainement, bien entendu, oui sans doute, volontiers, avec plaisir, mais oui, mais si?* They all know *non*, but can they produce *mais non, oh non, non merci, pas du tout, je regrette que non, à aucun prix, pas tellement, absolument pas?* And do they know the force of these and appropriate contexts for them? Do they have a wide enough range of adjectives of liking and disliking, so that they can go on from the simple *j'aime ça* to *c'est bien/pas mal/magnifique/extra/super*, from *je n'aime pas ça* to *c'est désagréable /moche/affreux/horrible/dégoûtant?* Variants like this with appropriate choice for context are the nuts and bolts of effective conversation: this is the stage to teach them explicitly and extend the simple, single expressions of the general course.

Oral production also needs to revisit areas covered in the early years of the language. It is easy to assume that because, in year one of the language-experience course, areas such as colours, clothing, foodstuffs, fruit and vegetables, and furniture were covered, that these are now known areas. In fact, a very limited number of items of vocabulary will have been learnt in those early stages, and if the area is not returned to there will be quite serious gaps.[6] It is not just a question of revision, it is also a matter of extending available material, principally vocabulary but also structures. A certain amount of imagination is necessary in producing material for 'revisiting': the fact that this is material of practical value is not enough to prevent a demotivating feeling of *déjà vu* ('Oh Miss, not buying a meal in a restaurant *again!*'). So some sort of a new twist is needed (catching out the dishonest waiter, impressing a new girl- or boy-friend whilst keeping them off the really expensive bits of the menu, working out a meal in the light of specific diets) to maintain the interest whilst adding layers of sophistication to earlier levels of performance.

Thirdly, it is important to extend oral production into new or almost new areas. The topic-based course will inevitably have covered only a limited number of areas in the time available and with a broader ability range to cope with; the early part of the specialist course will inevitably be concerned in the first instance with organizing the basic structure of the language in the pupil's mind. It is easy to omit inadvertently the next stage of extending practice into a whole variety of areas and giving the pupil the language material, especially the vocabulary, to do this. Here pairwork based on a labelled picture plus basic verbs and structures is simple to arrange and easily effective. We said in Chapter 2 that modern language teaching methodology is historically cyclical rather than linear, and here is an excellent example, since Comenius's *Orbis Sensualium Pictus* was based on just this method.[7] Admittedly the areas of interest have changed, and Comenius's picture of a fat knight in full armour (it could be Sir John Falstaff), surrounded by the aftermath of battle, might now be better supplanted by a Saint-Étienne football supporter on the terraces, surrounded by the detritus of modern packaging, but the principle remains identical. Such pictorial representations of language areas, presented orally in class, then worked out and extended by pair practice, are one way of developing oral production sideways, as it were, increasing the number of areas in which the pupil can perform without making his actual performance more sophisticated.

Finally we must return to the oral production of narrative, already mentioned on the first page of this chapter. The point of its importance has been made: how can we develop it? A simple way is the half-minute talk, done initially as classwork, then, to intensify the work, in pairs. Topics are set (different topics for As and Bs of pairs) based on language material very recently covered and the class is given ten minutes to prepare them. Notes may be made, but not continuous writing, and the notes may not be used during the actual narration. Then, once they have prepared themselves, individuals play the game of beat-the-clock: they simply have to speak continuously in French on their topic for half a minute *without any pause of longer than four seconds*. Comprehensibility rather than absolute accuracy is looked for, and a five-second pause represents a much greater sin than a wrong gender or an *être* verb used with *avoir*. Pairwork then consolidates this.

In this way pupils gradually build up the confidence to hold forth as well as to answer, to initiate as well as to respond. Gradually topics can be widened to cover areas that are not being currently treated in the course, but have been treated in the recent past, and the length of pauseless narration increased step by step from thirty seconds to a minute (a minute may sound nothing: in fact at this level in a foreign language it represents quite an effort of narration). Eventually, at sixth-form level, the same technique can be used unprepared.

Back in the fourth form, once the specialist course is well under way, English input to produce French output can also be introduced. We have discussed this in principle in Chapter 1, and its value as a skill in its own right.[8] By the stage we are now contemplating our pupils should be well beyond the belief that French is a coded form of English and that one-to-one equivalents are the norm. They should have enough of their own French to perform in it and, for such English inputs as 'Find out the time of the next train to Roubaix, book two return tickets and ask which platform', to trigger off French like *le prochain train* . . . *ça part à quelle heure?* . . . *aller-retour* . . . *et de quelle voie?* plus lots of *s'il vous plaît, monsieur, merci, ça fait combien?* and so on, in a variety of word-orders not by any means necessarily corresponding directly to that of English. It is of course important that necessary French is taught beforehand (do they know *prochain, aller-retour?* If they don't the exercise becomes nearly impossible) and that the necessary physical materials, here a timetable and ticket prices, are available and not so complicated as to detract from the efficiency of language practice. This sort of activity is ideal for pairwork, one member of the pair having the French information (in the example he is the ticket clerk with timetable and price-list), the other having a card or banda-sheet with, in English, the information to be extracted. Space on this sheet for the questioner to write down as laconically as possible the answers obtained (Here, 'Time of train = ..., cost of tickets = ... for two, platform number = ...?') can lend added point without wasting time and turn it into a first-past-the-post competition.

A written version of the skill of producing French from an English input can be built very realistically into civilization work, with the teacher giving the pupil a list (in English) of information for him to discover by writing to French sources (in French). We shall look at this in more detail later in this chapter.

So, considerable expansion of aural comprehension, expansion of written comprehension, extension of oral production into new areas and the development of the narrative skill and of foreign language response to English input. What then of the Cinderella skill, writing, at this level?

There is, by this stage, just one practical use for continuous writing and that is for letters. The personal letter to the French friend, the letter of thanks to the French family for hospitality or presents, the letter to make arrangements with a hotel for rooms or with a family for a visit, the letter of enquiry to the *office de tourisme*, to a youth hostel, to a campsite, to a villa-letting agency, to a car-hire firm. The letters that may prove useful divide into two obvious types, the personal and formal, and the latter in French presents (as with notice-comprehension in German) initially impenetrable forests of stilted, stylized prose. In fact there is a reasonably limited number of set phrases to be learned for formal communication, mostly at the start and the end of the letter, and once it is clear whether the context demands *merci de ta lettre, je vous remercie de votre aimable lettre* or *j'accuse réception de votre communication* the actual range of opening and closing phrases necessary (as opposed to possible) in order to produce various levels of formality is limited. None the less it makes sense to concentrate initially on the informal letter, both because it can be seen as of more immediate value and because it corresponds more closely to the register of French encountered through the other skills. If pairing of individual English pupils with French ones has been possible through *correspondance sonore* in the earlier years, now is the time to change to written correspondence. It is very difficult to establish a French pen-friendship from scratch that does not fairly rapidly wilt; it is much easier to continue through letters a friendship already begun on tape, with a person the pupil feels he already knows.

As with the other skills, classroom practice needs to be dovetailed to reality; the basic content of a letter established on the blackboard through class contribution and based on some current local event of general interest can form the core of some of the early letters of individuals. Given a standard beginning and ending and the class-developed material, the individual can then add a little of himself in writing and produce quite a respectable and comprehensible letter from an early stage. But one of the great problems of foreign-language correspondence is always 'What do I write about?', and as with *correspondance sonore* having specific information to elicit (again, the pupil focus is on message rather than medium) makes the exercise both more real and easier. Both informal and formal letters can be dovetailed to reality through civilization projects.

Letter-writing apart, writing also needs to continue as a reinforcement of work in the other skills (though there is even less excuse for busy-work writing in the specialist course than there was in the language-experience course), moving towards free composition, of which the letter, formal or informal, is of course a special case. Telling a story in writing is a perfectly legitimate letter-writing skill; it can also act as reinforcement to an orally narrated story. The fact that it also appears in many examinations at 16+ as a test in its own right may make us include it in the course on those grounds also. But for whatever reason we include it and in whatever form, 'free' composition needs to be heavily guided. A composition returned covered in red ink tells us more of the teacher's inability to judge pupils' levels and to prepare work effectively with them than of the written-language ability of the pupils. Nor should the free composition be over-used. The first two years of the three-year course should still see a preponderance of non-written work with limited simple written reinforcement, in order to enlarge the basis of acquired usable language. Only in the third year is there any real justification for enlarging the amount of written work in order to prepare directly for the examination. Many of the 'second level' drop-outs from modern languages at age 16 are a product of a diet of stultifyingly dull and obviously pointless written work in the third and fourth forms, included simply as examination preparation.

So much for the balance of skills within the course: how do we get our pupils to accept this and work for these ends, without which acceptance little or no learning will take place? The exam-passing motivation is there in the pupils from the moment they start on the specialist course, and to some extent it will carry them through. We are dealing now with young adults who are beginning to see the point of working towards a long-term aim. But without any intrinsic value perceived in the course this will on the way produce a deep cynicism about language learning ('We're really learning to pass the exam, aren't we, Miss?'), and rightly so.[9] How then can we build in a deeper, more valid motivation? In part by explaining our methods in terms of our aims to our pupils. A narration exercise, set as an exercise, will prove fairly difficult to get off the ground (it tends to produce a laboriously translated piece of written prose which is then read, or learned by heart and parroted). With the linguistic objective carefully explained and an atmosphere created in which we, teacher and taught, are working together for something of clear value to the taught, things become far easier. The view of a French lesson as some arcane rite, sometimes amusing, sometimes not, is far too often allowed to arise because the class really do not know *why*, in their terms, events in it occur. First-year children will accept the events for their own sake if they are interesting and varied enough; pupils at the level we are now dealing with will not.

But complicity isn't really enough. The perception by the pupil, every day, that what we are doing is really allowing him to speak French better in order to serve his purposes certainly means relevance of material, but it also means a further development of those purposes. A pupil with no interest in France can hardly be expected to make the French language his own; he can hardly develop a 'French' self if he has no knowledge of and involvement with France. Over these three years, and especially in the first two before external examinations begin to loom largest in terms of motivation, the role of civilization is vital, central rather than peripheral to the language-learning process. Again, as with the language-experience course, this should be no abstract study, but tied to personal experience. If anything it is even more vital at this level, as the pupil strives to develop mastery, that he should have reason and opportunity, face to face with the reality of France, to exercise his partial mastery.

It is neither practical nor desirable to build up this specialist course towards a single period spent in France, as we recommended with the experience course. Whereas that visit could be seen as a culmination and the end-point of growing linguistic knowledge, time spent in France should not now be an end-goal but an everyday (or at least an every-year) part of the language-learning process. The pupil should have a whole series of self-tests against the French environment. The exchange visit is the most exacting test of one's other, 'French' self, and this should certainly be part of the course in the second or third year; but at least one other school-organized visit should take place in the first year, and pupils should be encouraged to add as many personal or family visits as possible to this. The view that a holiday in France is a purely middle-class prerogative is rapidly dying, thank goodness, with travel plus bed and breakfast package holidays, in Paris particularly, currently on offer at astonishingly cheap rates.

But school-organized visits and exchanges are an essential part of the course, not an extra, and they should fit into a civilization programme of which they form an integral part. A programme planned over the first two years of the specialist course, covering a topic a term, could look something like this:

1st term: *Family life* — pulling together and extending the material from the language-experience course.
2nd term: *Aspects of French society* — work, sport, holidays, religion.
3rd term: *Regional geography* — starting from the 'twinned' region, then going on to other areas that individual pupils have had experience of, setting both these in the context of the Paris–provinces dichotomy.
4th term: *Money matters* — how money is earned and spent at different social levels. The values attached to it by society and by individuals in France.
5th term: *French history* — the trick here is not to fall into the trap of rehashing the history of France badly and boringly, but to take figures at the interface of French and British history and look at them from the French viewpoint (William the Conqueror, Joan of Arc, Napoleon . . .). This can be a tremendous eye-opener to pupils.
6th term: *The French political scene* — avoiding too much detail of party politics, but looking at where *power* lies in France

in contrast to Britain, what its limits are and why; considering especially the role of the President of the Republic and the relationship of central and local government.

Such a programme could be based on pairwork or groupwork and use as its resources both teacher-provided material and material sought out by the pupils, from the twinned French school, the French assistant, personal French sources. The teacher-provided materials need to be largely in French, but at a level where gist-reading is possible. This may mean adding side-vocabularies or in some instances doing a simplifying rewrite. Needless to say, such materials, though up-dated from time to time, are not expendable and need to be kept and gradually added to from year to year.

Specific projects relating to this programme and to school-arranged visits need to be developed. What form these take depends on particular circumstances: for instance, a regional geography project in term three can centre on a questionnaire which entails discovering what is special in the region, what makes it different from the rest of France. It can also include background not just from that term but from the 'aspects of French society' topic and the 'family life' topic, and perhaps in such things as regional food and drink draw on work from the language-experience course, at least as a starting point. The constant intermeshing of this civilization work with France and with real people in France is vital to keep the language work related to reality in all four skills. If in the course of his civilization work a pupil has to write to an *office de tourisme*, listen to a tape from his 'twin' in the French sister school, ask a set of specific questions of the French assistant, derive information from a file of original French printed material on a particular topic, borrowed from the teacher, the language work assumes a direct personal relevance; this is then extended many times over on his visits to France, especially those with a work programme organized by the school. The civilization programme itself forms a direct practice preparation for such visits.

With such a programme of language and civilization as that outlined above it is not difficult to keep pupils motivated in a course which is clearly designed to give them French as a usable tool and to show them ways and (most important) offer them opportunities to use it. Towards the end of the fourth form, however, the examination itch begins to develop. However carefully the teacher keeps past papers from the pupils, knowledge of them and of the areas of competence needed passes down the grapevine. Pupils become less ready to accept the relevance of anything not tested at O level, CSE, 16+. This backwash from the examinations is wholly regrettable, especially in view of their limited value as a test of the balance of skills we have advocated; however, it exists, and if we put pupils in for examinations we have a duty to them to help them pass them. In fact, a programme such as that outlined covers all the skills needed in the examination at 16, with the exception of translation into the foreign language and dictation, where these still exist; it does of course cover a good deal more besides. And since no board (except the Welsh) now actually *demands* a prose translation at O level, this can certainly be avoided: there are, as we pointed out in Chapter 1, very few things to be said for it in relation to the sort of aims we propose.

If we are to direct our pupils specifically at the existing examinations in this fifth year, then it seems wise to separate the skills more and to practise tests of those skills similar to those applied in the examination. With some regret one should also de-emphasize (though not drop) those parts of the course which are not externally tested. Actual past papers the teacher should hold back until the point is reached where, when she introduces them, pupil reaction is 'But they're quite easy, aren't they, Miss?' (assuming that that point is actually going to be reached!). She needs to build up pupils' confidence that they can pass the examination easily, not so much on the basis of the specific examination work in this fifth year, but on the basis of the real French they know they have learned over the previous four years. The conspiracy between teacher and taught to ensure that pupils pass the examination must never go so far as to devalue those four years' work that went before.

In fact, the essence of the examination year is the building up of confidence, both the confidence of pupil in teacher and the confidence of pupil in his own abilities. The former is a question of presentation, of always knowing, or appearing to know, exactly what you are doing and why. Qualities of efficiency and organization in the teacher, always important, become especially so in the examination year. Building up the pupil's confidence means making consistent demands on him, but always being careful to make demands that are not out of his reach; it means strongly rewarding good work and greeting bad work with disappointment but also with the confident statement that better is possible. Everything should be geared to pupils being encouraged to make the extra effort to surpass themselves. Teachers who start with (or at any rate express) the attitude that 'I can't see how any of you lot will pass this examination in a thousand years' find themselves to be all too often startlingly accurate prophets. A course of the kind described produces a stock of confidently deployed skills on to which examination techniques can be readily grafted.

So far we have considerd a specialist course that builds on experience of the same language gained in the language-experience course, and assumed this to be French. But what if, at the third- or fourth-form level, the language changes, or, alas increasingly rarely these days in the state system, a second foreign language is started? To what extent do aims and techniques then need to be different?

Not greatly, in fact. We have somewhat less time, though the two-year specialist course from scratch in German or Spanish is mercifully on its way out and an assumption of three years can be made much more readily for a second foreign language *ab initio* than for a continuation course in French. We also avoid the problem of the 'bridge' course in the first two terms that we saw as probably necessary in French, since we are starting from the beginning anyway, though we must naturally make different assumptions from those we made at the start of the language-experience course. Our students will, we hope, have learned what learning a foreign language entails, the sort of correspondence problems between spoken and written forms that may arise, what basic grammar terms mean and which may be generalizable. They will not be so dismayed by pronunciation and intonation differences, written accents, lack of one-to-one correspondence between languages. Where they will differ from the French *faux débutants* will be in not having the feeling of covering partly familiar ground, of systematizing and extending known material, and thus the early stages will be slower than those in French. But then, the second foreign language teacher will say, we have always faced these last points in teaching German or Spanish. Why can we not simply continue as in the past? Things do not need to change the way they have in French, surely?

Here lies the danger. The necessary, often painful, rethink in methods that the comprehensive school and French for all brought to the early years at least of learning French has hardly been felt in German and Spanish. Relatively very able children who have already done well in French are still the German and Spanish constituency, by and large. And with a limited range of available textbooks the tendency is to continue with an approach that often owes much more to the Grammar-Translation method than to anything later: certainly not to a method chosen with communicative ability as a prime aim.

In German particularly, with its extensively redundant morphological markers and its complicated literary syntax, the temptation was for teachers to say: the grammar is really very complicated; we have limited time; let us sacrifice the spoken word (partly or largely) and concentrate on getting the grammar right. In this they were not helped by a generation of textbooks, many still in use, that made the *necessary* grammar seem complicated by including, for the sake of completeness, much unnecessary grammar.[10] A small example: the *-en* adjective ending in *die alten Leute* is redundant in both spoken and written German. Plurality will be shown in many other ways, the *-n* is hardly audible at speed, in reading comprehension the *-n* contributes nothing. The common mistake of the foreign speaker of German is to say or write *die alte Leute* by analogy with *die alte Frau*. In the past, and far too often in the present, much valuable time was spent correcting this 'error': orally the correction had to be by a distortion of the pronunciation to stress the *-n*: '*die alteNNNN Leute*'. This example could be multiplied many times in German where much teaching still remains bemused by morphological niceties and learning bogged down in lists of verbs that take the dative, or the formation and use of genitive relative pronouns, or mnemonics for those masculine nouns that form their plural in *-er*, and so on. For communication these things are not important.[11] Luckily most Germanists or Hispanists also teach French and many could benefit from a transfer of methods and above all *objectives* from those that they already adopt in French. It seems particularly important when starting a new language at 13 or 14 to maximize efficiency and lay the stress from the start on aural comprehension with a quickly widening range of input materials, oral production at a lower level[12] and systematic reading comprehension. With a highly inflected language like German it is vital to distinguish *in the pupil's mind* between explanatory grammar ('this is why that is said like that; it would be nice if you could get it like that too, but it really doesn't matter if you don't') and necessary grammar ('you've just got to get this word order right or they won't understand you'). Very often in German the two correspond to morphology and syntax, and in the past far too much time has been spent aiming at totally accurate spoken and written morphology in German, at the expense of the much more important syntactical accuracy and general fluency. With examinations at age 16 in the form they currently take, it is no doubt wise to give some additional attention to written morphology in the third year of the course. By this stage, given the confidence born of a certain level of personal fluency, the feeling of despair that attacks German learners faced with its grammatical complications is far less likely to strike. This is an important point: it is much more likely that a pupil learning German will give up early than one with the same linguistic ability learning French because of the feeling that on the one hand there is far too much to master and on the other that he really daren't say anything in the language to communicate. In fact in the first year of the course we need more situation work than in French, to correspond to what was done in the language-experience course in French. We need far less stress on accurate production according to the rules than in the past, in order to build up confidence in the pupil's ability to communicate fluently at these simple levels. Above all we do not want at any point to imply that German or Spanish is going to prove more difficult to master than French. In fact, both German, with its similarities to English, and Spanish, with its similarities to French, are easier in their early stages as a second foreign language than French was as a first.

So, whether we are dealing with a continuation of the language begun in the language-experience course, or starting a new one from the beginning, we need to see our objectives as a combination of confident, fluent, fairly accurate oral performance, a confident, wide aural comprehension ability, a parallel, somewhat lesser ability in written comprehension, and some writing ability at a much lower level. This should then be realistically topped up in the final year with specific examination preparation. In classroom terms it means much more stress on listening, more stress on speaking, with pairwork that grows less and less tightly structured, systematic development of silent reading (starting, in the second foreign language, towards the end of the first year) and very much less class time spent writing than in the past, especially in the first two years of the course. It means a more relaxed attitude to grammatical 'mistakes' and much less stress on the intricacies of unnecessary grammar. And it means constant contact with the foreign country.

Such a course, as well as being self-contained and a valuable achievement in its own right, will also be an extremely solid basis for sixth-form work, at any rate of a certain kind. It may also encourage more pupils to believe that success is possible in foreign language learning, that speaking to foreigners is not so difficult after all. And feeling that they have really made progress and achieved something, they may also feel they could do more if they took the subject further in the sixth form or its equivalent. Alas, all too often, even though these sorts of emphases have been paramount within the pre-16 course, the new sixth former finds himself (or most frequently herself) in another world in which language learning, far from being a continuation of what has gone before, has suddenly turned into an abstract game with arcane rules. The sixth-form course has proved less susceptible to change than modern language courses at almost any other level, and for many sixth formers the work they are expected to do and the skills learned are entirely dysfunctional.

However, even here changes are afoot, as we shall see in Chapter 6.

Footnotes

[1] A better way of viewing them than drop-outs.

[2] The author's own course *Tout compris* (Oxford University Press) is such a course: however, he promises not to mention it again.

[3] This may be a good point at which to anathematize the 'grammar notebook', produced by the pupil laboriously copying grammar notes written up by the teacher on the blackboard or even dictated by her. This antique busy-work practice is regrettably still found here and there. Whilst writing something down of course helps to fix it in the mind, the time needed for such grammar-note copying is enormous, and totally indefensible in a four or five periods per week specialist course over two or three years. It is a marvellously easy way of filling time for the lazy or incompetent teacher, since the class can usually be persuaded that they are doing something useful.

[4] For an interesting discussion of the different processes involved in production and comprehension, see D. Slobin's excellent book *Psycholinguistics* (Glenville Ill. 1979) p. 43 et seq.

[5] Needless to say, the apparently casual 'package' has been carefully put together by the teacher to be within the competence of the class.

[6] This point can equally be made in subjects other than Modern Languages. How many pupils leave school with a far more simplified, unsophisticated, garbled view of, say, the Romans than of the Industrial Revolution simply because they studied the latter topic at 16 whereas they did the former at 11 and then never returned to it?

[7] Unfortunately, only on this. Comenius's approach in this book looks suspiciously like an early example of a language-learning panacea.

[8] See p. 18.

[9] Wilkins in *Linguistics in Language Teaching* looks at this point in some detail and concludes that 'All the most recent research agrees that it is the integratively motivated learners [i.e. those involved in the language rather than just learning it to pass an examination] who are the most successful.' Wilkins D. A. *Linguistics in Language Teaching* Edward Arnold 1973.

[10] *Mea culpa*: the author's 1960s' German course *Sprich mal Deutsch!*, though by no means the worst offender in this regard, shows quite a few examples of this. His 1980s' course, *Kapiert!*, hopefully proves that even course-writers are capable of learning!

[11] The author is reminded of an East German *Anglist* friend on his first visit to England who came in one day looking distinctly pale, saying 'I have just heard someone split an infinitive!'

[12] In the early stages the combination of these two in 'comprehension' exercises consisting of a passage plus German questions expecting German answers, itself a product of the Direct Method, seems rather dubious. It assumes virtual parity of ability in comprehension and production, which is neither likely nor desirable, as we have seen.

6 Modern languages in the sixth form

The changing nature of the customers for modern languages courses at 16+ has been obvious for two decades. Back in 1968 the Modern Languages Association was pointing out the need for at least three different types of sixth-form course, for specialists, non-specialists, and beginners[1]; two years later the Schools Council Working Paper No. 28 further divided the first category into those ending their language studies at A level and those continuing them at university.[2] To these groups we would now have to add: O-level failures retaking; CSE passes taking O level; groups working to a one-year sixth-form examination course (CEE, for example); groups taking specialist courses such as AO courses in French for Business Studies; groups working on the modern languages component in the General Studies course; groups studying the AO language-with-literature paper and primarily concerned with translation, and possibly linguistically completely unqualified groups simply sheltering from the cold wind of unemployment outside full-time education. Very few schools indeed could cope with all of these as separate courses, and indeed some of the strongest arguments for the establishment of sixth-form and tertiary colleges have centred round the varied nature of modern post-16 students and the range of their demands. What a sixth-form language teacher is much more likely to find allocated is a couple of periods of 'resit' work, no facilities for non-specialist continuation or beginners, perhaps a token period or two of General Studies French, and a so-called A-level course whose students are drawn from an ability band ranging from potential As to those who will certainly never make an E. It is none the less more than likely that this A-level course will bear a very close resemblance to the old grammar school course, with emphasis on prose translation, literature, and written French. Pupils will be expected to have undergone a miraculous transformation during the summer holidays from anxious fifth formers trying to cope with a whole range of examination subjects to dedicated literary academics with a feeling for the *mot juste* and an eclectic interest in European literature. They will find themselves with seven or eight periods per week, perhaps four of which will be devoted to a slow reading aloud and translation of a classical tragedy, one to prose work, one to unseen translation, one to essay preparation or the occasional dictation, and the additional eighth period to 'conversation' with a bemused fellow-pupil and the newly arrived French assistant in a cupboard by the art-room stairs. It is safe to assume that for none of the group, potential As or certain Fs alike, will this reality correspond to what they had hoped for or envisaged when they set down 'French' or 'German' as one of their sixth-form choices. The result has been clearly described by Her Majesty's Inspectors: 'The usual picture [of the typical comprehensive school languages sixth form] was of ill-read students with limited initiative reaching only poor to mediocre standards'.[3]

We explored some of the reasons for the continuation of this way of teaching in Chapter 1, ascribing it largely to a combination of conservative teachers and unchanged examinations, but what alternative can be suggested within the practical framework of staffing, timetabling and available resources?

Each of the two years of the A-level course needs to be viewed separately. O-level and CSE resit classes are clearly different in kind from the rest, and the work done in these classes is not an advanced sixth-form course. These apart, it should be possible to accommodate a variety of continuation courses and the first of the A-level years within the same framework if areas of common ground and common objectives can be identified. Let us then try to specify in what ways advanced courses ought to differ from the pre-16 specialist course.

Firstly, the two receptive skills should be removed from the sphere of French-for-foreigners to that of French-for-the-French. Aural comprehension should, by the end of the first-year sixth, be not just of the French that a French person produces to an obvious Englishman, but of that which he would use to a compatriot. Written comprehension should not be of specially written simplified French, or doctored real French, but of the undoctored printed word in its everyday manifestations.

To this might be added, secondly, the use of the spoken word not just for everyday exchanges but to begin to express *ideas* at some depth, to put forward *opinions*, to sustain *argument*. And lastly the written word should now take on some additional importance, with the production of reports, accounts, précis, greater attention now being paid in both these productive skills to increasing though not pedantic accuracy.

To sustain motivation across the range of ability we are likely to encounter in the modern first-year sixth, presentation materials need to be imaginative, immediate, various, and intriguing, and exploitation work must be individualized to give even the weakest some feeling of personal achievement and allow the most gifted to move ahead at something like their own pace. What sort of materials are appropriate?

The first stage is, surely, to scrap the first-year sixth study of set books. It was never very realistic to expect a new 16-year-old sixth former to plunge into French or German classical literature and to gain any real appreciation of its aesthetic or humane values. She would have read only a limited range of her own language's literature and have a very limited frame of reference for the new material. Interpretations, ideas, opinions expressed were inevitably second-hand. But even these small assumptions may no longer be made. For many, perhaps most of the present lower sixth the main, virtually sole, source of information and aesthetics is the television. Their out-of-class reading, if any, will be largely limited to the paperback bestseller list and the pop music magazines. Their background in English literature will be sketchy and include next to nothing from centuries earlier than this one. Nor will most of them read the serious press. Should we really then attempt *Horace* or *Goriot*, *Götz* or *Bergkristall* with a class who have no background in Shakespeare or the nineteenth-century novel, who have little or no direct experience of English literature? In the past, of course, the tendency was often to start with something more modern, and to go on to the classical set texts later: sensible enough, but there is no guarantee that the more modern book will be all that easy. There are two problems in fact: the lack of an English literature frame of reference (how is a German Romantic poem different from Keats? What makes Balzac's approach different from Dickens's?) and the lack of sufficient competence in reading comprehension to cope with the text as consecutive material for extensive gist reading rather than line-by-line translation. Paradoxically, our new sixth former may very well be better equipped than her predecessors in this last area, if she has been taught on a pre-16 course such as the one we have described in which the silent reading skill has been developed and practised. However, by postponing the set texts until the second year of the sixth, we can both extend the reading skill further during the lower-sixth year, taking it into more literary areas, and we can gradually introduce, through short and initially simple texts, some training in literary appreciation, so that by the second year of the sixth form our students approach the set texts with the confidence born of organized experience.

Postponing the texts until the second year means, too, that those students who are studying English Literature at A level will have made some progress in this area by the time the French set books are reached; for those who are not, a reading programme in English, set up in consultation with the English department, to key in with the French texts they will eventually be studying, is also possible during this first year.

Finally, the postponement of foreign literature until the upper sixth means that we can more readily accommodate in the lower sixth those pupils who wish to continue their language work for one year only: our lower sixth becomes a language sixth, our upper sixth a literature-plus-language sixth.

Having freed all seven[4] lower-sixth periods for language work, how do we organize them? Let us consider first the reading skill and the printed word input.

In point of fact at this stage reading, extensive reading that is, divides fairly clearly into two types: imaginative and factual; in concrete terms, say, the paperback novel and the news magazine. We can usefully approach the two in different ways. Our students will already, from their lower-school experience, be used to reading regularly. The fortnightly reader period on a library basis, with encouragement to read at home, will have given them considerable silent reading competence. The jump from, say, doctored Simenon to the paperback novel is, however, considerable, and it is unrealistic to expect the lower-sixth student to make this jump without help. To simply say, 'Look, there are whole rows of *Livres de Poche* in the library — go and start reading them now, instead of readers', will be quite unproductive. We need, for the first two terms, to earmark one of our seven periods per week as a library period, to take the whole group to the modern languages section of the library and *show* them the *Livres de Poche*. We need to help them choose one on the basis of their personal interests and then to be on hand to help them with their difficulties. The first real book in a foreign language that one reads is always the most difficult, the first few pages of that book the real watershed. It is here, however much reading comprehension has been practised in the lower school, that a very great deal of help will be needed. However, once this barrier has been surmounted, the combination of the regularly-timetabled period in the school library and the presence of the teacher always quick to help means that gradually speed is picked up and real reading for pleasure in the foreign language begins. With increasing confidence the pupils can be encouraged to continue reading their library books in their own time: by the end of the first two terms at least five or six should have been read by each pupil and discussed critically with the teacher. From this point on, novel or play reading can continue in the pupil's own time, with the occasional check by the teacher to satisfy herself that it *is* continuing, and the library period reabsorbed into general class time.

Factual reading is best approached through real French materials: photocopied articles from newspapers and magazines and other printed realia. One way to do this is to link the work in topic areas — drink, elections, Paris, women in French society, or whatever — and for the teacher to collect and have available material on these topics. Modern sixth-form textbooks also tend to favour this approach. It has a good deal to recommend it, but it does have the disadvantage that much of the material will have been covered already at a simpler level in the lower school civilization work and so the approach will lack novelty.

A more motivating method is through 'integrated events'. The materials the teacher needs for this are regular copies of a French news and picture magazine such as *Paris Match* on a fortnightly basis, with preferably one copy per pupil each fortnight.[5] She also needs a long-wave radio that will pick up a good signal from France Inter[6] (not difficult this: it is a very strong station) and a cassette recorder. And finally she needs her own English newspaper.

The French evening news bulletin is recorded regularly and stored for a couple of weeks. When the magazines arrive, articles that mesh in with already recorded news items are discovered and for each issue two topics at least are decided on. The teacher then uses the stored audio tapes and the magazine article (usually, but at this stage not necessarily, in that order) as the basis for the topic work. The item or area of news will be fairly current and the pupils will already have seen it in their English newspapers (and here the teacher's English newspaper will come in handy for those who haven't). The different treatments of the news item on the French radio, in the English newspaper, and in the French magazine can be discussed; then the French assistant can be brought into the act, with a more personalized viewpoint. For this the students can be set to prepare 'interview' questions to put orally to the assistant, based on what they have learned from tape and magazine, and a dialogue stimulated in which initiatory questions and viewpoints come from the students (they will be based of course on the tape and magazine input material, even taken straight from it — this doesn't matter). Written reinforcement then comes from, for instance, a two-column list prepared by each student of points for and points against in a controversial argument, or a written précis of a more factual item, or a summary of a personal viewpoint.

Variety is as important in the sixth form as elsewhere and so this pattern should not be slavishly kept to. The magazine can also be used as a basis for practising narration through short talks, with each student speaking on a different, prepared topic based on a magazine article for two minutes only (this time span can gradually be lengthened) and then answering one single question from each of her classmates (this ensures that they listen!) and from the teacher. The magazine can also be used for some translation work into English. At this level this seems a legitimate exercise for the student to extract more precise meaning from the French than her more usual gist-reading provides. It can also develop awareness of stylistic differences: in a magazine such as *Paris Match* there is a wide variation between the styles of articles, leaders, photo-caption articles, and advertisements, which the student can attempt to capture in her own English version. Magazine articles, too, can be set for homework study and then used as a basis for pairwork discussion (one member of the pair needs a sheet of leading questions to put to the other: if she gradually forgets to continue with these, so much the better, but they are a necessary fall-back).

The radio tapes are equally susceptible of a variety of different types of exploitation. Initially pupils at this level find a French news broadcast difficult to follow. A banda-sheet of difficult phrases worked through after the first hearing, followed by two more hearings, will make it considerably easier (again, as with reading comprehension, much depends on the amount of practice of the skill that has already been included in the lower-school course). The tape can be used for simple French question and answer work, or pupils can each be given an item to listen to especially carefully and take notes on (liberal use of the tape-recorder pause button is necessary) and the news sequence then reconstructed orally around the class. Obviously, many news items can also be starting points for civilization work.

The real point of both tape-recorded radio news and the French magazine is their immediacy. The pupils know that they are dealing with something that has just happened, that is real, that may even impinge directly on their own lives. Where the French assistant can also be recruited to add her own personal comments and to be questioned the sense of reality of the material being studied is further enhanced.

The obvious drawback to all this is the impossibility of planning exactly the year's course in advance. What, for instance, of the grammatical structure?

There is in fact a good deal to be said, at this higher level, for reverting to the explanatory grammar approach of the language-experience course of the early years. At that stage only grammar necessary to demystify the input material was taught. During the specialist course to 16+ we have given the students a basic grammar framework. Rather than follow this with organized grammar of a more and more recondite kind (with, say, pattern drills based on *ce à quoi je pense* . . .), it seems sensible simply to take points from material as it arises and drill and extend these if they seem worth it. It is true that there may be important major areas uncovered or only partially covered in the pre-16 course (the subjunctive in French, for instance), and some specific grammar work *may* need to be done on these; but generally anything that is really important will turn up in the aural and printed inputs, given the amount of presentation material we are using, and can be treated when it does so. Major surveys of areas such as the subjunctive can then be left until the second-year sixth, when we shall have in all probability fewer (and more academic) pupils left[7] and those pupils will during their lower-sixth language course have met more examples of specific uses of the subjunctive.

So here we have an approach that combines realistic aural and written input with oral output and some written output in various ways. There are a number of additional activities possible and necessary at this level. Students should obviously be encouraged to work on their own towards their own private goal of greater mastery of the language: pupil autonomy is one of the aims of any sixth-form course. To this end a bank of audio-cassettes that the student can take home and listen to is essential: it is an unusual sixth former these days without access to a cassette-recorder of some kind. The cassettes need to be properly catalogued and, quite essential this, a help-sheet provided with each, giving an introduction to or summary of the contents in English and a French/English vocabulary of difficult key words. If the cassette material is directly relevant to the student's civilization work, so much the better. Secondly, video-cassettes. It is now becoming possible to build up a bank of video-cassette material on France from various sources, and with the number of homes with a video-recorder growing rapidly, plus the possibility of a sixth-form video-playback facility in school, video-cassettes can be used for private study work at least with pairs of students. Obviously they can also be used from time to time with the full class for input, and this is especially relevant for civilization work.

There is one further area that it is valuable to cover in this sort of course, and that is an approach to literary appreciation. This, manifestly useful as preparation for the second-year sixth's literature course, is not quite so irrelevant to a first-year sixth language course as might be thought. Introduced in the final term (when an extra period per week is available, the former library period), it consists of a gentle, soft-sell approach based on material that all the group will have covered ('You've all read that book by Mannfred Hausmann, I think, at some time in the last two terms. Do you remember this passage I've copied? Let's read it again. It's a very important point in the story. How does he actually get that tremendous effect at the end . . .?'). With this approach it becomes an extension of the silent reading work to increase appreciation, at the same time giving a greater ability to see more deeply into the next work read.

A great deal of the work in a course like this can and should be conducted in the foreign language. Some of the translation work, grammar explanation, and literary work of the kind mentioned in the last paragraph needs to be in English to be efficient and effective. But the rest can be almost entirely in French and indeed should be: it was (is!) one of the curious characteristics of the old-style sixth-form course that work with pupils who were probably the most able linguists in the school was carried out almost entirely in English.[8]

Where does our relationship with France come into all this, that all-important end-product: language use *within* the civilization? Clearly in the contact with French everyday life through radio and magazines, through video, through the assistant; but what of direct contacts with the country itself?

Ideally, the summer term of the first year should be spent in the foreign country. The present author has in fact arranged term exchanges in this term of the lower sixth on an individual basis with notable success for the participants: but it is usually impractical to arrange such exchanges for *all* the lower-sixth students. It should not, however, be impossible to arrange an exchange visit in the summer between lower- and upper-sixth years for virtually all language students who are continuing for a second year in the upper sixth, and to combine this with a project to be pursued in France. The project should be decided on individually by the students and may well arise from one of the topics treated in the magazine and tape work. It should be prepared for by writing to bodies in France that can produce reference material and should involve interviews (perhaps based on prepared questionnaires) whilst in France on the exchange. It can be written up immediately on return. If the French A-level syllabus in use is that of the JMB or the SUJB, such a project can form the basis of the 3000-word dissertation that may be submitted as part of the examination. Whether it eventually forms part of the pupil's A level in this way or not, the exchange visit plus the project should be treated as one major end-product of the first-year sixth course. It should be supplemented, as before, by as many organized visits to France as possible, and where these are not possible the occasional 'language weekend' or 'language day'[9] is a good second best.

So much then for the first-year sixth language course. Where do we go from here? It is a reasonable assumption that we are only going to be left in the second year with A-level candidates or aspiring A-level candidates. An incidental virtue of the lower-sixth course outlined above is that, because its content is current and a good deal of the work is individualized, it can be followed for two years in succession (timetabling permitting) by a student who wishes to continue her language for more than one year without continuing to A level: this decision need not be made until the end of the first year. What though of our A-level candidates? Recently the question of 'which A level?' has assumed a much greater importance. Until the late 1970s there was not a great deal to choose between A-level examination boards, give or take a multiple-choice aural comprehension here or a dissertation there. But now London, Oxford and the SUJB are offering a language-based A level, with either no or virtually no literature, and other boards may follow suit.[10] So the possibility of setting up a non-literary A-level course based on language and society now exists. For many pupils who will not study the language beyond A level and for those who will go on to a language-based course at the newer universities or at a polytechnic this could be a very wise choice; for those students who intend to continue with a more traditional university course, perhaps less so. Problems of what and how to teach are greater with the old-style course, so let us for the moment assume that we are working towards a traditional language and literature A level.

Clearly our first priority in the second-year sixth must be the study of the set books. We must also introduce prose work, whatever our A level, since even the new language-only papers mostly include the prose.[11] We probably also need some dictation practice, and towards the end of the year some practice in examination technique based on past papers. But it is the set books that loom largest.

Our students are not entirely unprepared, however. They have been reading French novels regularly, as well as French magazines, and for the last term of the lower-sixth year they have been involved in some very simple literary appreciation work. It is a good idea, in the last weeks of the lower-sixth summer term, to hand out the easiest of the set books that have been chosen, preferably a modern novel, and ask the students to read this simply for gist as they would any other modern novel, in the course of the summer. In that way we can start on our first set book immediately on their return after the summer holiday with everyone having read it through once.

It is wise at this stage to devote four of the seven periods that are presumed to be available to the set books. Line-for-line translation is always to be avoided, and with a novel is impossible anyway, but careful study of climaxes and crucial turning points in the book both in relation to character and plot development and in relation to the novelist's craft in achieving specific effects is important and will undoubtedly involve some element of translation. But the novel, like the other set books, needs to be seen as a whole, and discussion should centre particularly on the actions, characters, and values involved. One of the greatest uses of the study of literature, whether in English or in a foreign language, at this age of about seventeen especially, is as a surrogate for life, a way of experiencing emotions, relationships, values at one remove, of setting generalizations from literature against new, particular experiences in life.[12] Set books should be chosen with this aspect in mind, as well as for the more obvious reasons (such as a balance of plays, poetry, novels, or because the teacher herself is enthusiastic about them). It is this direct relationship to pupils' own lives that needs to be stressed when dealing with classical literature especially, rather than formal aspects such as special vocabulary or the mechanics of the alexandrine.

Plays may be read aloud in class, or better, arranged as a rehearsed evening play-reading. Sometimes it is possible for the upper sixth to present a dramatized play-reading (effectively a performance with books) of a shared set book to the lower sixth. A good preparation for this is to dub a record of the play (one of the *Sélections sonores Bordas*, for instance) on to cassettes with one role suppressed, a different role on each cassette. Pupils can then practise reading their parts against professional French actors. All this helps to get a feeling of the structure of the play and above all its effect in stage performance.[13] Obviously, if an actual professional performance can also be seen, so much the better.

If a poetry collection is to be studied, this can be linked with the textual appreciation lessons that were started in the last term of the lower sixth. They should gradually develop into simple *explications de texte*[14] and the poems from the collection used as well as others. Pairs of poems on the same subject contrasting in style are a good way to begin to appreciate what each poet is really saying and what feelings he wishes to express, and to analyse the craft that he uses to produce this. One small plea here: when a poem has been taken to pieces and examined, don't forget to put it together again: the pupils' reaction to the final, uncommented reading by the teacher should be much more meaningful than the first time the poem was read.

Some literary and social background work will be necessary — it is difficult really to appreciate Molière knowing nothing of Versailles, or Hugo knowing nothing of the French classical tradition — but this should be kept to a minimum. Self-contained values should be a criterion of choice of a set book: a book that can only speak to us when its whole historical context is known is not ideal for study at A level.

The second new element is prose work. However good a test prose translation is, and it is perhaps not really so good as some of its proponents have suggested, as a skill it is of very little use in its own right. The A-level prose, however, is not something that can be done well without a good deal of practice, and we would be wise to devote one of our weekly periods to this. D. O. Nott suggests an effective approach to prose work via aural comprehension.[15] This consists of playing a taped version of, say, a short newspaper extract (about 150 words) and, having explained the vocabulary, giving out an English translation of the text. The students are given time to underline phrases that they cannot translate, then the recording is replayed in segments of three to five sentences each (too long for the students to write down the segment in full). Students are allowed to note down in French those phrases they have managed to spot at the end of each segment. The replay is repeated, twice if necessary, then students write their prose translation. Nott observes that this not only produces fewer mistakes than the traditional prose, but also prevents word-for-word translation, with students becoming aware of the different ways in which an idea may be expressed in the two languages. Indeed parallel work, initially by direct retranslation — French to English and back to French again — then by choosing proses and translation passages within the same topic area, is the most effective way to build up prose work. The prose period is also the place for the periodic survey of grammar areas which have not yet been covered in an organized way, as well as for revision of grammar points that are revealed as not well known by the translation work into the foreign language. This last is in fact one of the few real virtues of prose work.

We have so far used up five of our seven periods per week allocation of time in this second-year sixth, and the remaining two periods must be used for realistic input and related output in the aural-oral skills, with written reinforcement as in the lower sixth. We shall perhaps want to include some more sophisticated material from news magazines such as *L'Express* or *Der Spiegel*, but it is wise not to overestimate our pupils' ability or interest in the political and economic spheres: *Paris Match* can still be very valuable at this level. In this second year, written précis of articles can be developed into more formal essays, still on magazine and news-based topics, but involving the presentation of the student's own opinions as well as facts culled from the French sources. It is vital that during these two periods the aural-oral work is kept to the fore, with virtually no English spoken, since there will inevitably be a good deal of English used in the literature and prose periods.

The approach to sixth-form language studies outlined above is not by any means ideal. The second year looks somewhat unbalanced and really involves too much non-French work. This is of course because it is dominated by A-level papers which, largely, reflect the need of old-fashioned university foreign-language courses for students with some rudimentary literary knowledge and an ability to write prose translation. As long as this kind of university thinking dominates A-level syllabuses, they will remain dysfunctional for very many pupils. What we have above is perhaps the best compromise solution if we are to teach to the old-style A level: if we were to continue the sort of lower-sixth course we have advocated through the upper-sixth year we would produce better linguists but many A-level failures. The fact that most of the pupils who take A level have no intention of studying French literature and language at a traditional university is just one more example of the examination tail wagging the education dog. If we can accept the fact that, however much we ourselves may love the literature of France or Germany, analytical studies of the literature of a foreign country pursued either in English or in the foreign language are not an appropriate or meaningful activity for most of our sixth formers, then perhaps we shall be readier to make the radical break with tradition and offer our pupils one of the non-literary A-level syllabuses. In Chapter 7 we shall consider what these involve, look at other external examinations and explore modern languages testing in general in greater detail.

Footnotes

¹ *Modern Languages Courses in the Sixth Form* MLA Pamphlet 1968.
² Schools Council Working Paper No. 28 *New patterns in sixth-form modern language studies* Evans-Methuen 1970.
³ HMI: *Modern Languages in Comprehensive Schools* (op. cit.) p. 8.
⁴ Seven periods plus one period with the assistant is a common allocation. We have here assumed only the seven: this presumes that we shall be using the assistant's time largely in paired teaching, in the lower school as well as the sixth form. See Chapter 8.
⁵ One copy per pair will do if cash is very short. *Paris Match* offers special subscription rates for classes on an alternate issue basis.
⁶ France Inter broadcasts on 1829 metres on the long wave.
⁷ HMI found that 'in the first year of the sixth form roughly one in seven pupils was studying a modern foreign language and in the second year only one in ten.' Figures include resits. HMI *Modern Languages in Comprehensive Schools* (op. cit.) p. 8.
⁸ HMI, again, speak of a sixth-form norm of 'pedestrian, over-cautious teaching' with 'inadequate use of the foreign language, and this was particularly prevalent in advanced courses, at a stage when one might have expected the foreign language to be the principal vehicle of communication.' HMI *Foreign Languages in Comprehensive Schools* (op. cit.) p. 16.
⁹ In the former a residential hostel of some kind is taken over and a totally French atmosphere created, with films, games, etc., all in French and with a total embargo on speaking English. Cooking too should be done by the students themselves, also in French, and the washing-up! Staff plus assistant provide the language resource (*'Qu'est-ce que tu veux, Jean? Ça? Bien, ça, c'est une passoire . . .'*). The language day, usually a Saturday, can be run in the same way on the school premises, though the residential weekend is much more effective.
¹⁰ See Chapter 7, p. 116. The giant JMB, too, is about to produce (1984) a major new modern languages A-level syllabus with very much more stress on language, on oral work, and on school-based assessment.
¹¹ C. T. Gill Leech, a member of the London University working party which designed the new London examination, justifies the prose in these terms: 'Firstly, it was felt to be a legitimate test at this level of study; students should expect to be tested on their knowledge of the basic structures of the language. Secondly, it provides an objective assessment of their ability, as opposed to some other parts of the exam . . ., which will, necessarily, be marked on the basis of a subjective assessment.' Gill Leech C. T. 'French A level: the new "language only" syllabus of the London Board' in HMC Modern languages Report No. 2 *The Teaching of Modern Languages: a View for the 1980s* London 1980. Both arguments might perhaps be challenged.
¹² And, of course, it is not just *modern* literature that can provide this. One of the most successful set books the present author has ever taught to an upper sixth was *Andromaque*, simply because so many of that group were experiencing for the first time a similar emotional involvement to the one presented in the play, in some instances of the same triangular kind.

[13] This can be vital: a simple reading of *Mutter Courage,* for instance, produces a quite distorted effect of the play in theatrical terms and in terms of the balance of character and ideas because it virtually eliminates the vital role of Kattrin, Mutter Courage's dumb daughter.

[14] A useful book here for the teacher is Howarth W. D. and Walton C. L. *Explications: The Technique of French Literary Appreciation* Oxford University Press 1971.

[15] Nott D. O. 'Introduction to Sixth-Form Language Teaching' in HMC Modern Languages Report No. 2 (op. cit.).

7 Language Testing

'Finally the problem of oral and reading tests must be faced. Only a small proportion of our correspondents found time or facilities for these in any but the senior forms. Most teachers relied on dictation to test the oral work which had been done in the previous term'.[1]

'The basis of the group's thinking is that the prime purpose of foreign language learning is to be able to engage in communication. This view, which the group believes is widely shared by teachers, should determine what is to be tested and how it is to be tested . . . listening and speaking will predominate.'[2]

The first of these quotations represents virtually the whole of what is said on oral testing in a 450-page volume of guidance by modern language teachers for modern language teachers published in 1956; the second is taken from the outline proposals of the working group on modern language testing (at 13) of the Assessment of Performance Unit of the Department of Education and Science, in 1980. The change in attitude represented by these two quotations over a quarter of a century must be borne in mind when considering criticisms levelled at present-day testing practices in public examinations: the distance between the attitudes of teachers in 1956 and those of many teachers of today who would present language learning (and therefore testing) as primarily concerned with oral communication is enormous: if examination boards look conservative and, at times, amateur from the perspective of the communicative classroom, their comparative radicalism would probably have produced apoplexy in the authors of the 1956 IAAM volume.

In the simplest terms, language testing can be divided into tests of aptitude and tests of performance. We shall mostly be concerned with the latter in this chapter, but it is worth first briefly considering the former.

Until recently a pupil's aptitude for a foreign language was determined either by his general ability, as measured by a variety of IQ or verbal reasoning tests, or in the case of a second language by his performance in the first. In fact, specific language aptitude tests were originally developed after the First World War, along with other attempts at standardized tests, with only limited success. As

Carroll found[3], measured IQ and scholastic ability do correlate fairly well with eventual language-learning achievement, so that the old pre-comprehensive policy of giving foreign language learning opportunities only to the higher ability child has some apparent sense in it. What Carroll also pointed out, however, was that lower ability in this field really means 'taking a longer time to get to a particular level' — there is no evidence that anyone cannot learn a language, given sufficient time. Most work on language aptitude tests has been in the USA, and the best known are the Carroll–Sapon Modern Language Aptitude Test (MLAT) of 1958 and the Pimsleur Language Aptitude Battery of 1966. However, work at the University of York in connection with research into language-laboratory effectiveness in the 1970s produced a considerably better test, at any rate in measuring aptitude for learning German. It involves the making of analogies within the grammar of Swedish. This test has since been widely used in schools and has proved extremely reliable.[4]

Language aptitude tests are however of only limited use in the school situation. Who learns a first or second language is determined by a whole range of factors from parental choice to the number of desks in room 17. Testing for most teachers means either internal tests within the school or the system of external examinations that has grown up since, effectively, 1917 with the establishment of School Certificate and Higher School Certificate. It is this latter system of performance tests which dominates syllabuses, teaching, and methods and, quite often, determines by analogy everyday internal testing.

Public examinations in this country are a product of the mid-nineteenth century: in the 1850s the concept of merit as the basis of entry to the Civil Service, the universities, even the Royal Military Academy began to replace that of patronage. The effect on school syllabuses of the London University Matriculation Examination, by which in 1858 entry to the university was thrown open to competitive examination, was considerable; in the same year Oxford, Cambridge, and Durham instituted Local Examinations, the forerunners of the GCE boards. The London Matriculation in particular rapidly came to be seen as an examination of competence in its own right and a school-leaving goal, rather than simply as an examination for entry to the university.

By 1868 examinations in secondary schools were proliferating, giving the Schools Inquiry Commission of that year considerable concern; outside the schools such still-existing bodies as the Royal

Society of Arts or the City and Guilds of London Institute were setting up their own vocationally-oriented examinations. More universities instituted their own examining boards, including the Northern Universities' Joint Matriculation Board, and by 1911 concern at their further proliferation had produced another commission (the Consultative Committee on Examinations in Secondary Schools) and a further report. The recommendations of this report were implemented by the Board of Education in 1917, laying the foundations for the present O and A levels. What was set up at this stage was a system of just two examinations to replace the multiplicity: School Certificate, taken at about age 16, and Higher School Certificate, taken at about 18. The universities were to provide boards to run these examinations, and the Board of Education was to provide co-ordination through the Secondary School Examinations Council, the forerunner of the Schools Council. The School Certificate Examination was not offered in individual subjects but in prescribed groups of subjects, and by 1938, the Spens Report found, it had come to dominate entirely the work of the secondary grammar schools, in both framework and content of the curriculum. The postwar reforms in education, with their vast concomitant increase in the secondary school population, exacerbated the problem. In 1947 the Secondary School Examinations Council proposed the General Certificate of Education, a single-subject examination whose Ordinary Level pass was to be at a higher level than the School Certificate pass and which was not to be taken before the age of 16. (This latter requirement was dropped in 1952.) This new GCE O level was seen quite specifically as an examination for a small academic élite, with the rest of the school population catered for largely by internal school assessment. The O level was to be no more than a preliminary step on the way to A level.

It was not to work out this way. In parallel with the GCE O level, which came to be regarded as a suitable goal for most of the grammar school population and for some secondary-modern pupils as well, a whole series of more or less appropriate examinations came to be taken in the secondary schools as leaving examinations. Some of these were already existing public examinations, others were devised and run specially by local consortia, encouraged by Ministerial Circular 289 of 1958. The Beloe Committee, set up by the Secondary School Examinations Council in 1958 to investigate this growth, found that 43% of schools were entering candidates for examinations other than GCE[5], involving them in a vast range of local, regional, and national examinations, often at parental expense.

It was to bring order out of this chaos and to provide for the obvious demand that the Beloe Committee was led to recommend the setting up of a teacher-controlled single-subject examination for pupils at a level lower than GCE O level, with its own group of local boards, recommendations which were to be adopted almost unchanged to produce the examination for the Certificate of Secondary Education, revolutionary in its control by teachers and the possibility it for the first time presented of an examination directly related to the subject syllabus that had been taught. It was this aspect of the CSE, its relating an examination directly to the content of the syllabus taught, that can perhaps be seen as its most fruitful contribution — a step that led towards the precise criterion-referencing of the Graded Objectives movement. Its other revolutionary aspect, the production of a broad-based examination that was not simply catering for a small pupil élite, led in the direction of the single 16+ examination and a far wider degree of norm-referencing than that represented by GCE O level.

But CSE, as a by-product of Beloe's insistence on a teacher-controlled examination, produced a new range of examination boards, jealously independent of each other, to add to the existing GCE boards. So we have now seven GCE boards in England, the Northern Ireland, Welsh, and Scottish Certificate boards, and twelve CSE boards, all acting more or less independently. The examinations they produce in modern languages have been criticized for being by and large conservative, questionable in their appropriateness, vastly different from one another in what they test, often amateurish in presentation, and set and marked with a high degree of secrecy, not to say obscurantism, with regard to what is being tested and rewarded.[6]

At O level, most of the boards have no published syllabus, leaving it to teachers to derive a view of what will be tested from past papers, and where aims are stated they tend to be general and unspecific. Sometimes indeed the aims conflict with the facts, as with the AEB: 'in the examination great importance will be attached to the oral use of language' (45% of marks go to written French, 30% to translation into English, only 25% to oral use of language).[7] There is a move in all languages towards a closer definition of syllabus in terms of grammar, vocabulary, and topic areas, but the CILT team found that the majority of French O-level syllabuses (eight out of fourteen) were still completely undefined.

Some boards are secretive about the relative weightings they give to the different skills at O level, but most appear to give 20% or less to oral, 20% or less to aural, 30% or less to reading and the largest percentage to writing competence. There are exceptions (the B syllabus of the Joint Matriculation Board gives 49% of the marks to oral/aural skills), but even the most cursory review of the comparative mark weightings[8] for French shows that O level is predominantly still an examination of written skills.

The actual tests used also give cause for concern. At the level of detail there is often surprising carelessness in paper setting (for example, in one paper the Welsh Joint Education Committee demands that replies to reading comprehension questions in French be in the same tense as the question, then asks a past historic question *Qu'est-ce qui donna à l'enfant l'idée de manquer la classe ce jour-là?* that needs an imperfect answer, *Il était très en retard*). At the more general level it is the unnaturalness of the language used that is the most serious fault. More often than not examination boards set reading comprehension tests of gist reading material, then treat it as if it were intensive reading material. They use largely narrative texts, often literary, almost never natural, to test listening comprehension. 'As far as the editors have been able to discover, not one specimen of genuine spoken language has been set in a public examination. Few indeed are those pieces that have even been contrived to sound natural.' Orals rely on reading aloud, a skill quite different from the spontaneous use of the language, on 'conversations' that are 'not anything that would be recognizable in the outside world as a natural conversation'[9], on parroting, on descriptions of pictures and picture sequences. Tests, sometimes, do not test what they purport to — multiple-choice tests test discrete vocabulary items rather than gist comprehension, comprehension tests test production. Mark allocation is often impossible to discover unless one knows an examiner personally. Examination tasks at this level can be largely faulted for both their inadequacy and their artificiality. If the former is discouraging to teachers and candidates, the latter has a more pernicious effect. The teacher who did not consider the examination that her pupils must take in the year they were to take it, who did not prepare them for it by giving them practice in the tasks they were expected to be able to perform, could well be held to be failing to do the job she was paid for. This is in itself bad enough when the tasks are so unnatural and so unproductive. Frequently, however, the backwash is not just through all or part of the last year of the course. It is by no means unusual to find the last two or even three years, the whole or the greater part of the language-option course, devoted to tasks determined by the O-level examination. The boards have a grave responsibility here for shortcomings in language teaching. It is difficult to quarrel with the CILT team's conclusion: 'The general impression that arises from a study of O-level papers in modern languages is of a luxuriant tangle which has grown up in response to a whole series of different needs but which, as a whole, does not present a coherent pattern . . . Most of the tests as they stand are inappropriate to the emerging view of what language teaching and examinations are about. Over the past fifteen years there has been a good deal of tinkering going on, but the basic framework has often remained very much the same, as is shown by the almost universal use of picture compositions, dictations, and reading aloud which have been with us since School Certificate days.'[10]

At CSE and 16+ the picture is slightly rosier. More boards attempt to define the syllabus on which their examination is based; there is a greater willingness to use tests of communicative ability, such as role-playing; where Mode 3 is used teachers have greater flexibility in examining their own courses; and the relative mark weightings for the skills in Mode 1 are a little more realistic than those of O level (the majority of boards give 30% or over to oral, 20% or over to aural, 20% or more to reading skills). But the weight of writing is still astonishingly heavy, with one board (the Welsh Joint Education Committee again) giving no less than 42½% of the marks to the writing skill.[11] The same sort of questions arise as with O level about suitability of material and validity of tests, and there is a general air of even greater amateurism (characterized immediately on opening the papers by the low-quality of artwork used by some of the boards for picture essays). And though there is a greater willingness to define a syllabus, the syllabuses as defined often raise more questions than they answer, and sometimes reveal an odd mixture of principles underlying them. Take for instance the syllabus of the Joint 16+ examination in French, one of the more detailed. The syllabus is quite extensive and appears in general to put a premium on communicative skills; at the same time it includes such literary items as *ne . . .point* and *je puis* for recognition, without even mentioning, even for recognition, the orally extremely frequent conditional perfect[12] (I bet *you* wouldn't have done that!).

There *are* better tasks than those used by many of the O-level and CSE boards, and we shall be considering some of them later in this chapter; meanwhile it is difficult to avoid the conclusion that the multiplicity of boards involves a spreading of examiner talent too thinly and that more competent and more efficient examinations might be produced by a much smaller number of perhaps more professional boards.

In an attempt to bring the examination 'system' more into line with what teachers feel objectives should be, recent changes have been, paradoxically, in the other direction, with, in order to produce more functional examinations, a vast proliferation of local groups turning out graded tests almost as a cottage industry.[13] This turning away from the traditional examinations has two very important factors underlying it.

Both the O-level and the CSE examinations are norm-referenced examinations. Their aim is to spread candidates out in such a way that they fall in more or less appropriate numbers into the pre-ordained categories of the examination, and by definition at least half the candidates, very many of whom will have pass grades, must see the test as 'beyond them'. Also by definition such a test has to discriminate well between candidates, has to ferret out their weaknesses rather than reward their overall strength. The CILT team note that 'this preoccupation with discrimination is apparent in a great deal of the boards' comments on their examinations. Again and again we find that a test is approved of because it discriminates well, or was abandoned because it failed to do so.'[14] But of course the boards have to be thus preoccupied, by the nature of their examinations. The graded objectives movement gathered momentum towards the end of the seventies because teachers perceived that, to make what was learned relevant, a carefully prescribed area of knowledge and skills to be mastered was needed, and further, that such a prescribed area to be mastered needed a test that would represent a single hurdle to be jumped rather than a booby trap that would spread the bodies of the contestants around the course in a bell-shaped curve. A criterion-referenced test, in other words, like a swimming certificate or the driving test.

So the first factor involved in the move to graded objectives in modern language learning was the concept of a precise syllabus to be mastered and a pass/fail test that told you if you had mastered it. And not one pass/fail test, but a series of pass/fail tests so that you didn't have to continue too long to see whether a particular area of the syllabus really *had* been mastered.

But in many ways it was the second factor that was even more important, because such a scheme easily allowed, indeed almost demanded, that the syllabus be defined in terms of what the student should be able to do — in language terms, what he could understand and communicate. And it is this second factor that may ultimately prove the more important. The norm-referenced nature of O level, CSE, and (so far) 16+ brings with it a concern with form rather than message, with accuracy rather than fluency, with structure rather than function. The CILT report again: 'It is not what the language is doing or meaning which is of primary importance [in current examinations at 16+] but whether it is well formed. This leads to the contradictions inherent in so many of the tasks . . . Testing of formal elements is much easier to do. Mistakes are obvious to all, the marking can be much more objective and therefore reliable, and reliability is essential when discrimination is so important.'[15]

Having dropped the need for discrimination beyond the simple pass/fail level, the way is open to a fundamental change in what is examined from the form of the language to the ability to use it, from practice elements to performance, from knowledge of its parts to the employment of one's available language as a whole. It will not have escaped the reader's notice that this coincides with the stress throughout this book on the ultimate importance of that third stage of language learning, the student's autonomous use of language for purposes that he has made his own, to communicate and be communicated with.

The initial reaction to graded objectives and tests has been extremely positive both from teachers and from pupils, so much so that the more cynical have begun to whisper words like 'bandwagon' and 'panacea'. None the less, first research evidence is very much in favour. An evaluation published in 1981[16] covering pupils in Leeds and North Yorkshire showed the experimental pupils (those involved in work towards graded objectives) with very significantly more positive attitudes to learning French than the control pupils (those not involved in such work). This positive attitude embraced all ability levels and included those who actually failed the graded test. In addition, significantly more experimental pupils expressed an intention to continue with French the following year and reports from the schools indicated that they did in fact continue. Though the ability to reach a goal that is clearly defined and set not too far ahead must be an important factor in this positive view of graded French, the personal relevance of a syllabus expressed in precise communicative terms must surely be at the heart of the matter — 'Look, I can do something useful and I've proved it!'[17]

The graded test movement is not without its problems. It is unfortunately true that most graded tests have been used with less able pupils and classes, and there is a distinct danger that such tests may come to be seen simply as motivation for the slow learner. And they have yet to win general recognition outside the schools. A second problem is that, as we have seen, O level and CSE are norm-referenced examinations. How does one relate a criterion-referenced graded test to them? Whilst it is relatively easy to produce a criterion-referenced test that can be accepted as the equivalent to a particular grade at CSE, to extend this (especially to extend it in the direction of 16+, a norm-referenced examination 'for 60% of the population') within a norm-referenced framework seems difficult if not ultimately impossible.[18] Again, there is the danger of reduction: that what is defined as an output syllabus (what the pupil may be expected eventually to do) becomes accepted by the teacher as an input syllabus (all she has to teach). Finally, the proliferation of schemes inevitably brings with it the question of test quality: if the 22 CSE and GCE boards are too many to produce test materials of appropriate quality, is it not likely that the same criticism may eventually be levelled at the sixty or more graded objective groups? As a second stage of the movement some sort of rationalization and consolidation seems necessary.

If, within the lower school, there is a growing feeling of the inadequacy of the examinations at 16+ in terms of their content, their presuppositions, and their position at the end of a very long course, what sort of changes can we see at the sixth-form level? In examinations, as we saw earlier in Chapter 6 in methods and materials, we step back into the world of the *ancien régime* when we consider A level. For most boards little or nothing has changed over the past ten, twenty, thirty years even. Candidates are asked to translate into French, to translate from French, to write an essay in French, to write literary essays in English on four set books and to undergo a cursory oral examination, the latter averaging only 12% of the marks. The language tends to the literary, with the occasional nod towards dialogue and situations from modern everyday life. Nearly a third of the marks go on the literary essays.

For all the criticism that we have made of O level and CSE, for all their inadequacies, there has been some attempt made to view language as something heard and spoken and used to communicate. The average A-level examination views it as a form of communication virtually only within the narrow register of literary French.

The blame for this is usually laid at the door of the universities, and it is certainly true that the A-level course predicated by the examination forms quite a good preparation for a university French course that has a heavy literary weighting. Most universities do not want this to change, and many sixth-form teachers do not either. There is an interesting illustration of this. In the early seventies a quite significant event occurred. The Joint Matriculation Board, always an innovatory board in modern languages, instituted a number of changes in its A-level French examination. They were hardly revolutionary and were in fact largely concerned with offering an alternative to the literature paper, with texts on social and political background and extensive as well as gist reading. For a time, for instance, Brassens songs appeared on the set books list, and clearly a stimulating language-and-society French course could have been devised for both lower and upper sixths with this examination as its sanction. In fact the syllabus was discontinued in 1979 because of a lack of sufficient entries. It is, of course, the teachers, not the pupils, who decide which syllabus candidates shall be entered for.

One or two other minor innovations of this period have stuck. Listening and reading comprehension, tested by multiple-choice questions, were introduced by the Joint Matriculation Board and are now compulsory with three boards and optional with a fourth. The other boards still do not test listening comprehension. The Joint Matriculation Board salvaged from its attempts at change in the early seventies a 3000-word dissertation in English done in the students' own time as an alternative to *one* of the questions in the literature paper, and the occasional sociological rather than literary work is to be found in the set-books lists; but generally the average A-level syllabus has been a fly set in amber.

There are, however, changes afoot. Southern Universities Joint Board introduced an alternative non-literary syllabus in 1977 which included a 3000-word project not unlike that of the JMB, which abolished the prose and, most revolutionary, included an aural comprehension test of more than one Frenchman speaking something like real French; the paper also contains other more traditional elements. London and Oxford began work on new 'language-only' syllabuses and the first candidates for London's Syllabus B sat the examination in 1982. The London paper sets precisely circumscribed topics for study *(L'essor de l'industrie après la Seconde Guerre mondiale* under *Aspects économiques, Le Nord Pas-de-Calais* under *Aspects géographiques)*[20]. Gist reading comprehension and intensive reading comprehension are tested separately (the latter by translation into English); gist aural comprehension is tested. There are traditional elements still in the syllabus (translation into French;

reading aloud) and 35% of the marks go on essay writing of various kinds, but literature, apart from one literary/sociological subject among the topics for study, is banished.

In 1981 Oxford also announced a new language syllabus. This transfers set texts to the oral examination and treats them as subjects of general conversation rather than literary appreciation; it has a test of aural comprehension and no translation into French but remains a quite heavily written-word based examination. Also in 1981 a group of Hampshire teachers published a very detailed alternative language-based syllabus and examination[21] and the same year an ILEA working party submitted a further alternative syllabus, also language based. In May 1981, the JMB appointed a working party to carry out a 'fundamental reappraisal' of its modern languages A level; the working party produced a proposed new syllabus in 1984.

To an extent all this activity has been a result on the one hand of pupils arriving in the sixth form from a different background from the former five-year grammar-based course, and at the same time of the disastrous decline in numbers opting for the traditional A-level course. It has also, as with most reforms, been the product of a number of energetic, enthusiastic, and hard-working individual teachers who got up and did rather than simply complaining.

Among these various developments, one of the most closely reasoned and worked-out syllabuses is that of the ILEA[22]. This centres the work around topic areas, some open to the objections we made in Chapter 6 to this approach (such as the tired old *Les loisirs et le sport, Le transport* etc.), some (such as *La criminalité et la violence dans la société actuelle*) less so. The proposed examination tests all four skills, with listening and reading tested for both intensive and extensive comprehension. Though there is no literature paper, extensive reading is also tested on the basis of four books chosen from a list of eight (post-1870 and by no means limited to 'literary' texts), and two more books have to be read for the oral examination.

Listening comprehension includes radio-type news items, interviews, and group discussions, as well as narrative; candidates are asked to summarize in English where extensive listening is required, and to answer detailed questions in English where intensive listening is tested. The two and a half hour reading test paper is very much longer than the traditional A level: three *faits divers* of 800 words each, two serious articles of 2000 words each, and a 2000-word short story. The *faits divers* and the story have gist questions, the articles are tested for intensive reading.

The 'books' paper, called a 'reading programme test' to avoid the idea that this is literature, has a context question to be answered in French which demands a purely factual summary of events, and, rather oddly, a traditional literary appreciation essay in English on the fourth book.

Written production is limited to a quite realistic letter written in a carefully specified situation, and a rather traditional essay. The oral carries almost a quarter of the marks, lasts half an hour, including questions on books read, conversation based on stimulus material first seen fifteen minutes before the examination, and role-playing tests.

An A-level examination such as this is not only revolutionary in dropping translation into both French and English, literature, dictation, and reading aloud: in what it includes it should have not the negative backwash into classroom teaching that we have seen with the traditional examinations, but a positive effect. The stress on news items in the aural comprehension will bring French radio into the classroom, the nature of the reading paper will demand considerable practice in rapid extensive reading, the use of written French in the 'books' paper and the inclusion of books in the oral test should ensure that books read are discussed in French in class (and the dropping of literary pretensions here will make it realistically possible to do this). There are still some oddities left in this examination, but generally it is a sanction that would fit extremely happily with the sort of approach that we have described in Chapter 6.

There are signs then of quite exciting changes at the top of the school as well as the changes brought about by developing views of the nature of language learning at the bottom. Schemes such as the ILEA A level are probably more likely to be acceptable to the universities than possible higher-level graded test developments. One would like to think that the prognostications of the authors of *Graded Objectives in Modern Languages* were true: 'It seems very likely that the demand for a two-stage course in post-O-level work mirrored by these developments [in A/O courses and other sixth-form syllabuses] will grow. If that is so then these could well represent the higher levels of a graded objectives scheme — the ones that could be considered as university entrance qualifications.'[23] The suspicion of change and the slow progress in eroding the old dysfunctional examinations at A level makes the possibility of university acceptance of a graded test as a matriculation qualification look, alas, only too remote.

Testing, however, is not simply something that goes on at the interface between school and society; it is something we as teachers undertake daily, and it is worth asking ourselves whether the tests we employ in our everyday teaching are any more appropriate than the ones we have criticized in public examinations.

Until the sixties tests tended to be unscientific: written exercises heavily biased towards translation, gap filling, isolated sentences, translation of vocabulary items, with little concern for their direct relationship to what had been taught or for their reliability. This was followed by the objective-test movement, with testing of discrete items in the separate skills and a good deal of statistical analysis based on them. Objective tests tended to concentrate on what was easily testable[24] and ignored problems of communication and the interrelation of skills. Now in the eighties the communicative competence movement asks for a situational approach to testing, with as paramount the ability to communicate a message rather than reproduce forms, and with degrees of precision in communication as the criterion of success. In everyday testing in the classroom many teachers are still fixed in the first or second of these stages. Let us consider some appropriate testing strategies for the third.

Classroom testing is either for the teacher's or the pupil's benefit. Often it is for both. It represents feedback to both on what has been learned, what needs revision, what has still to be done. Much feedback to the teacher is informal — the teacher is constantly monitoring reactions — and indeed the more experienced a teacher is, the less frequently she needs to test formally: overtesting is a characteristic of new teachers.

In the first stage of the presentation of new material it is understanding and retention that we are most concerned with, and it is at this stage that comprehension tests will be used, largely of aural comprehension. It is important to isolate exactly what is being tested: open-ended questions to be answered in English may be testing a pupil's ability to write coherent English as well as his understanding of French; questions to be answered in French are even more obviously testing two skills at the same time. Multiple-choice tests, unless very carefully produced (and for everyday use multiple-choice test construction is a terribly time-consuming business) will only sample the comprehension of parts of the material and leave the teacher unsure of how much of the rest has been understood. A test comprising a series of true/false ·nts in English is much easier to construct, is easy to mark, ise so little writing is involved, is quite quick to administer.

121

Though not the only possible test (variety in testing material is almost as important as variety in teaching material), this sort of test of aural comprehension has a great deal to recommend it.

In testing reading comprehension we need to distinguish between intensive reading and rapid reading. For the former, photos of public notices, instructions from packets, record sleeves, 'how to use' notices — on petrol pumps, laundrette machines, coffee dispensers — all these can be used in their original form, as overhead projector slides or duplicated, and it is here, where specific information has to be conveyed, that translation or at any rate precise explanation in English by the pupil seems most appropriate. The same goes for the testing of intensive listening, less frequently needed than intensive reading perhaps, but still needed — reporting a telephone message exactly, giving details of a particular region's weather abstracted from a radio weather forecast, passing on timetable details given orally, understanding the important details in loudspeaker announcements — here again this is best tested by explanation in English. It is easiest to administer such tests in a written form, and incidentally this, the writing down of written details in English, is a very natural activity in relation to intensive listening.

Gist reading comprehension is best monitored by a private oral question-and-answer session on the book read when, during the silent reading period, it is exchanged for another. This is best kept informal (tell me about the book, what was it about, what happened then, did you like it, how long did it take you to read, what did you find difficult?). It will help guide the pupil towards a suitable next book and allow the teacher to monitor progress. If test of gist reading of other types of material is felt to be necessary — travel brochures, guide books, newspaper and magazine articles, and so on — the written summary or the oral report in English is most natural and effective.

The testing of production skills comes towards the end of a teaching sequence. In oral production we need, especially from the point of view of the pupil's perception of the test, to stress communication above all. In fact, of course, the teacher will want to have feedback on communicative ability, fluency (speed of reaction and production), and accuracy. Oral production is notoriously difficult to test. The classroom problem is not so much the lack of objectivity in assigning marks (the greatest problem with external examinations), since the testing is only for the one teacher and her pupils and can thus afford to be more subjective. It is the time taken listening to each individual. One partial solution is to involve the rest of the class in the assessment activity: for instance, the pupil being tested stands up and describes someone the class all know, or a film or television programme they have all seen, without mentioning the name, and the class have to guess who or what it is. The pupil being tested may in fact not know he *is* being tested if all the teacher needs is feedback. Alternatively the teacher can take over from one member of a pair during pairwork in order to test the other on the work being done, the rest of the class simply continuing to work in pairs. The French assistant can also be useful in oral testing: for instance, pupils go to her one after another with questionnaire cards, in English.[25] They have to elicit the various pieces of information demanded on the card in French, then make note-form answers in English. The assistant can grade the questioning for comprehensibility (and if required, for fluency and accuracy) and the English answers to the questions on the card will give a measure of the student's ability to understand the assistant's French answers as well — two skill tests for the price of one!

Whatever strategy is employed, it is important that a genuine task of communication should be involved, that communicative effectiveness should be marked, and that the pupil should realize that this is the principal grade given, since for him the end-point of the language learning process is its effective use. The feedback on fluency and accuracy is important to the teacher in deciding on revision and practice areas that are necessary for this or for all pupils, but for the pupil it is surely the ability to communicate that counts. The Scottish course *Tour de France*[26] includes speaking tests of this kind in its published material. For each point tested (e.g. asking what the price was, saying whether you can afford that or not, etc.) the pupil gets one mark if the message is conveyed comprehensibly, a zero if it is not. Errors that do not hinder or distort the message are accepted. Fine from the pupil's point of view, and these errors are messages about the pattern of future work to the teacher.

The other productive skill, written production, is easier to test. It is here that concern with form rather than message is still most prevalent. Teachers who want to lead their pupils to a real use of language orally and in the areas of reading and listening, still concentrate entirely on form when it comes to writing. There is in fact, as in spoken production, no reason why both form and communication should not be tested together, the pupil gaining marks for comprehensibility of material produced, the teacher also taking feedback for future work from the formal errors made.[27]

Writing a note for the French au pair, writing a shopping list, writing to a hotel or a tourist office for information, applying for a job from the *Figaro* small ads: this sort of task, at various levels, can be marked for the ability to convey information. Notice that when we reach the highest level the question of accuracy begins to be involved *within* the area of communication — a more accurately phrased letter, over and above the level of basic comprehensibility, may be more likely to produce the job interview. Form at this level has become functional!

A word should perhaps be said at this stage about the cloze test. Invented in the early fifties in America, it is a test of intensive reading comprehension and of written production at the same time. Words in a passage are deleted at regular intervals (say, every ninth word) and the candidate fills the blanks with the original word or an acceptable alternative. The first sentence of the test is often given in full to set the scene. Easy to set, easy to mark, apparently a very good measure of a candidate's general performance in the language[28] (form and meaning are both tested, as is predictive ability), it none the less leaves one with an uneasy sense of an artificial test unrelated to real activities and giving the learner no skill-related feedback, except perhaps the satisfaction of having completed a puzzle (or the frustration of not having completed it!). It is in current use, as far as the author is aware, in only two public examinations in modern languages in this country[29], though it is much used abroad. It should, one feels, be approached with caution and used with considerable discretion. *French 16–19* (op. cit.) sees it as a possible indicator or calibrator for general language performance as part of the A-level examination; here it may have a greater role than in the everyday classroom.

The above types of test are indeed a long way from most public examination tasks, and the fact that, apart from cloze tests, each of them gives the pupil direct feedback about his ability to convey or process information contrasts starkly with the public examination where all the candidate knows is that he has passed with, say, grade C. This tells him nothing of what he can actually do in real terms, and it tells him precious little in comparative terms.[30] There is, however, the alternative of graded tests where these exist, and it is of course always possible to offer a Mode 3 syllabus and tests of one's own, and not just in CSE, based on tasks that are more realistic and skills that are more usable. And finally one should remember that if public examinations are as they are, it is because a sizeable proportion of the teaching profession wants them to be so. Nothing better illustrates the conservatism of modern language teachers than the fact that, two decades after the prose became an optional part of the O-level examination, the majority of candidates are still entered for it!

Footnotes

[1] IAAM *The Teaching of Modern Languages* University of London Press 3rd edition 1956 p. 136.

[2] Assessment of Performance Unit *Foreign Languages* Department of Education and Science 1980 p. 3.

[3] Carroll J. B. 'The Prediction of Success in Intensive Foreign Language Learning' in Glaser R (ed.) *Training Research and Education* University of Pittsburgh Press 1962 p. 122.

[4] See Green P. S. 'Testing for Language Aptitude' *NALA Journal* 8, 1977 pp. 51–5.

[5] Ministry of Education *Secondary School Examinations other than the GCE* (Beloe Report) HMSO 1960 p. 11.

[6] In the section that follows I am greatly indebted for factual information to the CILT publication *Modern Languages at 16+* (published in 1980 by a team led by Alan Moys). The secrecy and lack of coherent dissemination of information by the various boards makes collection and comparison extremely difficult, as the CILT team found: 'In amassing this information the editors have been obliged to consult sometimes as many as thirteen sources for one examination. The average number of sources consulted for GCE boards was 7.3 and for CSE boards 5.7. This situation makes it very difficult for teachers to inform themselves adequately.'

[7] Moys A. *et al.* (op. cit.) p. 245.

[8] Ibid. Table 113.

[9] Ibid. p. 266.

[10] Ibid. p. 270.

[11] Ibid. Table 113.

[12] ASLEB/JMB/TWYLREB/YREB *Joint 16+ Examination French Syllabus* 1979.

[13] By the end of 1982 there were more than 60 such groups in the country, 23 of which had already produced CSE Mode 3 submissions (*GOML Newsletter* 7 November 1982 p. 2).

[14] Moys A. *et al.* (op. cit.) p. 268.

[15] Ibid. p. 269.

[16] Buckby M. *et al. Graded Objectives and Tests for Modern Languages: an Evaluation* Schools Council 1981.

[17] It is beyond the scope of the present volume to analyse individual syllabuses; Harding A. *et al. Graded Objectives in Modern Languages* CILT 1980 is a good starting point for this.

[18] The York Area grade 4, for instance, has been accepted as a CSE Mode 3, but has had to be tested in such a way as to produce a norm-referenced spread as required by CSE grades. The whole principle of the test seems to be compromised.

[19] They were no doubt influenced by Schools Council Working Paper 28 (op. cit.), which proposed amongst other things a sixth-form A-level course

centred on extensive reading. The working paper, greeted as seminal on its publication in 1970, in fact seems to have had very little effect on sixth-form practice.

[20] The Associated Examining Board also prescribes social topics, but these are merely the basis of one question in the literature paper.

[21] *French 16–19: a new perspective* (op. cit.).

[22] For fuller details of this scheme and its genesis see Murphy P. 'Objectives and Methods in the design of an alternative 16–18 examination' in Lunt H. N. (ed.) *Communication skills in modern languages* CILT 1982.

[23] Harding A. *et al.* (op. cit.) p. 89.

[24] Note for instance the stress on pronunciation tests in Lado R. *Language Testing* McGraw Hill 1964 (a standard work). As late as 1977 in Valette R. M. *Modern Language Testing* (2nd edn.) Harcourt Brace p. 97 tests for 'comprehension ease' are single item vocabulary tests from a discrete group (numbers, colours) rather than tests of true comprehension. And if the 'pin-pointing' technique of objective testing has questionable validity, it should also be remembered that multiple-choice testing can only begin to be effective in the two receptive skills: production must be tested in other ways.

[25] 'What is the assistant's father's name? Is he still alive? Where does he live? What does he do? Has he ever visited England?' and so on.

[26] Scottish Central Committee on Modern Languages *Tour de France* Heinemann Educational 1981.

[27] The progressive marking scheme of the former West Yorkshire and Lindsey Regional Examination Board in its written papers may be mentioned here: anything written which, when said, would sound correct *is* correct. So *je suis allé* or *aller* or *allez* or *allée* are all correct. This is at any rate a step along the road to marking principally for communication.

[28] See, for instance, Rankin E. F. 'The Cloze Procedure — its Validity and Utility' in Farr, R. *Measurement and Evaluation of Reading* Harcourt Brace Jovanovich 1970 pp. 237–253, and Davies A. 'Language Testing: Part 2', *Language Teaching Abstracts* vol 11, no. 4 1978.

[29] In the Oxford Board's new language-only alternative A-level examination; and in the JMB's O-level German, Syllabuses A and B, as an alternative to translation into German.

[30] As the CILT team once again put it: 'How can one equate an Oxford [O-level] candidate who has passed an examination where 12% is given for oral competence and 19% for written composition with a Grade 1 CSE candidate from the Middlesex Board where 35% is given for the oral and 25% for written composition?' op. cit. p. 268.

8 Classroom aids

We have now considered the gamut of secondary teaching from first to sixth form, looked at objectives and their appropriateness, and considered approaches that offer realistic possibilities of attaining these objectives. In this and the next chapter we are going to review some of the physical means at our disposal inside and outside the classroom to help us achieve them.

Over the last thirty years the modern languages classroom has been transformed. In the average school it consisted then of a blackboard, a dais, rows of individual desks, and little else. The dais has gone, the blackboard though still there may be used for many things other than written language, and the individual desks with attached benchseats will have given way to tables arranged so that pupils can work in pairs. There are probably posters and photos of the last trip abroad on the walls, together with examples of pupils' written work, of materials sent from the French sister-school, and with luck there may be an overhead projector and a tape-recorder as fixtures on the teacher's desk, together with two good quality extension speakers in the corners of the room facing the class. And the average lesson in this room will find the teacher deploying some or many of a wide and rewarding variety of aids. Let us consider these, beginning at the beginning of the teaching sequence with aids to presentation.

We are presenting a language, and at the initial stage we are offering a model for pupils to imitate. Our own French may or may not be near-perfect, but even if we are bilingual our French may not be standard (whatever that means!) and we should want to offer a range of voices to correspond at least in part to the reality the pupil is going to encounter in France. In the early stages of language learning the audio tape-recorder, the obvious choice of aid, is not as useful as might be expected. We have already mentioned children's reaction to it in the NFER primary French investigation,[1] and there are two apparent reasons for this. One, which we often underestimate, is how many meaning clues a tape-recorder deprives us of. However good the reproduction system (and some classroom systems are not all that good) there is distortion and loss of clarity; the audio recorder also deprives us of the visual situation and the facial and bodily reactions of our interlocutor. Furthermore, that quality of the tape-recorder for which it has often been praised, its ability to present an utterance over and over again without modification of speed, stress, or intonation, can at this stage be a real disadvantage. A teacher, perceiving a learning problem, will repeat, altering speed, stress, and intonation as appropriate and the pupil will, in many cases, then understand. This is of course what we do in real life when asked to repeat something our interlocutor has not understood. The tape-recorder does not — cannot — do this. So, at a time in the early weeks of learning when pupils are struggling to get to grips with all the various aspects of the new language, the tape-recorder, unless judiciously interrupted, may in fact offer a further problem rather than a solution. Audio-visual presentation helps to some extent by adding some visual clues; video-tape presentation helps still more, and with video presentation the frozen frame allows work on a just-heard structure to be developed before allowing the tape to continue; but the question of clarity remains. Easier than either to understand is presentation by the teacher in tandem with the assistant.[2] This needs careful preparation to ensure that what is presented corresponds to the teacher's intentions — an obtuse or imperceptive assistant can be a disaster. The greatest problem for the teacher of her own language in the early stages of her career is to realize what is easy and what is difficult in it. The assistant, unless helped, tends to see all problems as vocabulary problems, and to view syntax and intonation (often the greatest stumbling blocks to comprehension) as unimportant. Given careful joint preparation and the initiative held, especially in the early stages, firmly in the hands of the regular teacher, the combination of reality and authenticity on the one hand and clarity and flexibility on the other makes the assistant as a presentational aid hard to beat. It is very easy to adapt most two-person dialogues in courses with audio or audio-visual presentation in this way, and the assistant can then be deployed for continuation work within the same lesson by splitting the class into two groups, the teacher taking one, the assistant the other, and thus doubling the time available for controlled repetition work.

However, there is at most one assistant per school in any language, and much of the time a teacher must perforce be teaching alone. Audio and video-tape can be helpful here; so too can realia.

The fact that teaching with objects has been around for some little time[3] does not make it any less valuable. The nearer the classroom comes to the French reality, the more practice can be seen to approach use. The can, the carton, the bottle, the box, the coffee cup, the filter, the sugar cube, and so on, all help to put language learning into a context of relevant civilization, to link learning directly to reality. They need to be kept up-to-date (what more depressing than a dusty camembert box?) and handy (constantly lugging a bagful of objects to school on the bus in the rain is discouraging), but they should be seen as a first-rank visual resource. And they can be deployed to bring not just visual reality into the classroom. Making a vinaigrette sauce with olive oil, mustard, and wine vinegar brought back from the summer visit to France, then allowing the pupil to try it with *julienne* carrot-sticks can be the source of valuable language work *(ajouter, mélanger, battre, goûter,* use of *on)*, realistic civilization work, and noun vocabulary taken directly from the bottle labels. And it extends the palate as well as the mind.

The flashcard, though easier to carry, is usually a second-rate two-dimensional substitute for the real French object. This is not to dismiss the flashcard. It depicts things that cannot be brought into the classroom and has possibilities of symbolism that the real object lacks and which are appreciated by the young teenager. *'Il est petit, il est grand'* can be done with objects or with pupils; but even more memorable is

Flashcard I **Flashcard II**

il est petit *il est grand*

Flashcards, like realia, serve the purpose both of presentation-clarification and of recall-trigger. The more memorable the trigger, the more memorable the word or phrase associated with it.

But flashcards are not there simply to be held up by the teacher to illustrate or trigger items of vocabulary. Positioned around the classroom they can symbolize places or categories and can be used for semi-realistic simulation work: the classroom becomes a town with flashcards symbolizing places — the station, the main square, a restaurant, the church, the tourist office. Or it becomes a supermarket, with the flashcard of a baguette symbolizing the bread shelves, that of a pork chop the meat counter, and so on. Getting to places, deciding what to do there, shopping for a meal, and finding out where things are in the store — simulations such as these can easily be developed with half a dozen flashcards round the room.

A pack of flashcards can be used for slot substitution work orally; blu-tacked to the blackboard in the appropriate slot in a written sentence they can be used also for written substitution work. In games a flashcard chosen at random by a pupil and then concealed can be guessed by the rest; instructions related to a flashcard hidden in the classroom can be given and followed; one of a large number of displayed flashcards can be described by the teacher and the card guessed by the pupils, and so on. Flashcards have a whole range of uses at all stages of the teaching process. For some (not all) of these purposes cut-outs are even better.

Cut-outs lie half-way between flashcards and realia and serve a similar purpose. With a little blu-tack attached they can be stuck on the blackboard and form a movable part of a drawing; they can equally be stuck on to posters, on to other objects in the classroom, even on to people! Clothes cut-outs can be hung on a chalked washing line on the blackboard, packed in a bag, given to people to 'wear', put on display in a 'shop', taken to and collected from 'the cleaners'. Only a limited suspension of disbelief is needed and our presentation and early stages of practice come quite close to reality and genuine communication about objects in situations.

Slides, posters, and filmstrips offer more detailed presentation material than a flashcard or series of flashcards, but their essentially static nature tends to generate noun vocabulary plus adjectives rather than verb use. The partial black-out needed for slide and filmstrip means that they have to take up a major part of a lesson for the hassle of setting-up to be worth while; if however a major part of the lesson is to be spent in semi-darkness and relative passivity the visual content of the slides or filmstrip has to be very compelling indeed. It rarely is, and this has undoubtedly been a factor in the demise of the audio-visual course.

Better than these, because much more flexible and easier to set up — it needs no black-out — is the overhead projector slide, to which overlays of static or moving objects can be added. This gives both the large-scale detail of the poster and the mobility of cut-outs or realia. By means of small flaps with sellotape hinges, static elements can be added to a picture, gradually building it up. Equally, elements can be removed, producing, for example, a variant on Kim's game, pupils having to remember what has disappeared. This latter technique is also a particularly easy way of producing a cloze exercise on a text. What is apparently a continuous text is projected: in fact the words to be clozed have been written on a separate overlay slide. This is then removed, leaving a text with blanks, and the pupils' task is to reconstruct the whole text. Moving figures — cut-out paper silhouettes sellotaped to long strips of acetate — can also be easily produced for the overhead projector. A town map with movable silhouettes of a policeman and running criminal superimposed can, for instance, be the basis of a series of verbs of motion plus *à droite, à gauche*, etc., as well as involving the noun vocabulary of streets. This combination of detailed background slide and superimposed motion is one of the most useful aspects of the overhead projector employed for visual presentation.

Sixteen-millimetre film is of little use for presentation, at any rate in the early stages of learning. The problem is not the limited material available or the setting-up difficulties, so much as the poor quality of foreign language film sound in an ordinary classroom. The microcomputer, too, in its present stage of development is of little value to presentation work. Schools do not yet have sufficient computers to allow presentation work with individuals, and presentation to a class or even to a large group nullifies the computer's main value, its interactive nature. It also deals essentially only with the printed word at the moment. Although the combination of video-disc and computer allows non-linear access to presentation materials of both audio and visual nature, there is no available modern languages software of this kind at the time of writing and few schools have the necessary hardware. Most commercial computer software in modern languages has to date limited itself to the more obvious areas of grammar and vocabulary, with programs largely of a testing nature and then mostly based on grammatical perceptions of the printed word and printed recognition vocabulary. Much more will be possible when the video element can be linked on an everyday basis, but even then the computer is likely to remain mainly a reinforcing agent of the passive skills rather than a means of presenting new material.

What of aids to practice? For a couple of decades the most expensive aid at the practice stage, the language laboratory, has gradually been losing favour. Partly this has been due to its unreliability, so that a good part of a laboratory period has often been spent trying to cope with non-functioning equipment; partly too it has been the lock-step nature of the materials used. Marketed originally as a way of individualizing learning, it has proved in practice to be rather the reverse. Because laboratory work of some kind has to be done if a class is timetabled in the language laboratory, especially if the laboratory is of the permanent, non-transformable kind, the weekly period spent there tended to impose a pattern on the rest of the week's work. And the usual necessity to put material out from console to booths at the start of each laboratory period meant that work was not done at the pupils' pace but at the pace of the tape being put out. Add to this the fact that in the early years at any rate the laboratory was largely used for mechanical four-phase pattern-practice drills, which pall and bore even if some of the material practised is subsequently incorporated into genuine communicative work, and it becomes clear why a regular laboratory period each week taken from a total of perhaps four for the language came to be seen as hardly the best way of using the available time. Schools still using the laboratory tend now to concentrate on aural comprehension, with a tape-plus-worksheet format, often on a library basis, with pupils listening individually to the tape as often as they need before embarking on the worksheet testing tasks. But it must be admitted that ordinary cassette-recorders with headphones would do this job just as well as the complicated interactive machinery of the audio-active laboratory at a fraction of the cost and with much greater reliability.

The overhead projector can of course be readily used as a source of quite varied visual cues for oral practice. Masking and flaps are useful here to reveal more and more of the material already on or hinged to a slide, to produce sequential responses from the class within a fixed pattern; the moving figure again can be used in the same way as in presentation.

For written practice the home-made spirit-duplicator worksheet is much in favour. At its best using a variety of colours, an interesting layout, and cartoon drawings it can be extremely effective, not least in that pupils see it as something produced especially for them by the teacher, something more personal than the textbook exercise, and often more precisely suited to their abilities and needs. However, it is important not to overuse it — it may well be that the jolly worksheet handed out by you to 3Z in period eight French is the eighth jolly worksheet handed to 3Z that day in eight successive subjects. However dazzlingly produced yours is, it will not have any great motivational effect.

Worksheets or cards can also be effectively used to produce pairwork oral practice, and used in this form are unlikely to reproduce types of work done in other subjects. Each member of the pair has to have a different but complementary sheet; or a single sheet can be folded to allow only the appropriate half to be seen. Cues to stimulate the dialogue can be in English, in picture form, or a mixture of these two; or one interlocutor can have a set of proposed questions and possible answers in French whilst the other merely sees information (a bus timetable, a street-map, a picture, a menu) that enables him to answer these questions. At higher levels dialogue cues can be in the foreign language.

Flashcards can also be used at the practice stage, principally as cues in slot substitution drills, but also, reproduced in quantity as a homework task by pupils, as cues in pairwork drills. Such pairwork cue-cards, kept and sorted by vocabulary areas, can be used over and over again for a whole variety of pattern drill substitution practices.

The foreign assistant, too, can be just as useful at the practice stage as at the presentation stage: producing the stimuli for chorus responses whilst the teacher gets in among the pupils to monitor these responses more effectively, or working with one half of the class whilst the teacher works with the other in the same room, or helping to control pairwork, or stepping out of a teacher/assistant dialogue to practise items *(Qu'est-ce qu'elle m'a demandé? Et qu'est-ce que j'ai dit . . . ?)*

The computer comes a little more into its own at this stage, both to provide enrichment practice in the form of an animated worksheet for the more enthusiastic to work on in their spare time, and also as re-explanation and practice for pupils who have been absent, in fact or in spirit, when work was done in class. Of the four language skills, reading, intensive reading that is, is really the only one so far directly available through the computer — typing in the foreign language beyond the simple *oui/non* or ABCD of a multiple-choice response can be unproductive and time-consuming, in the lower school at any rate. This means that even here at the practice stage the computer is only of limited value, but some practice software material for this stage *is* now becoming available.

When we reach the third stage, that of language use, it is realia that are most valuable as aids — buying drinks, shopping for food, booking in at a campsite, are all more effectively done if real materials are there to be used. Pairwork sheets and cards as more open-ended stimuli are important, and groupwork games using cards or boards or bingo-type materials can be an excellent way of stimulating pupils to use the foreign language (careful devising so that the game is both simple and linguistically productive is necessary: as is policing to see that enthusiasm for winning does not lead to use of English rather than the foreign language). Computer language games played in pairs can stimulate oral use of the foreign language between the participants in a not dissimilar way. Since however this is usually own-time work, monitoring is difficult. This sort of work is perhaps better kept for the higher levels of the language course where motivation can be to some extent assumed and pupils retain a continuing awareness that the oral French generated between them is a large part of the object of the exercise.

The assistant as a resource for information-gathering specific to particular tasks is invaluable at the stage of communicative language use. The asistant can tell the pupils about actual everyday French reality in a way that they can directly compare with their own reality: the way a day's work and play is divided up, the layout of a French flat, the furnishing of a French living-room, what goes into a French kitchen, the important places in a French town, the way that national holidays are spent, how to make an apple pie, how important family relationships are, the current expectations in table and social manners — all these things and many more can be effectively personalized by the assistant where they are necessarily generalized by books or the teacher. She allows pupils access to real French life. In asking the assistant questions and establishing comparisons with the English facts as the pupil knows them, genuine curiosity is stimulated and met, and real communication is taking place. And at higher levels civilization tasks can be set that involve finding out from the assistant as well as from books and other printed materials, with real communication involved that uses all four skills.

At all levels, then, and at all stages of the teaching process, language-teaching aids are a necessity rather than a luxury and their imaginative use a clue to successful teaching. In that they bring a measure of reality into the classroom they have a strong motivational effect. In that they add a dimension to classroom communication they move us more than a few steps towards our goal of true communication in the foreign country. It is this latter that must always be our ultimate target, and it is with means to achieve this that our next chapter is concerned.

Footnotes

[1] Burstall C., op. cit.
[2] We shall have a lot to say about the assistant in this chapter — properly used she is the teacher's most valuable classroom aid. Paired teaching with the

assistant is beginning to be seen as a highly valuable, though still underused activity, especially in the early years of the language. The HMI *Survey of the use of Foreign Assistants in the Sheffield Metropolitan District* (DES 1983) found 10% of assistants' time overall devoted to this (too little, the report implies) and judged 'some of this joint work was very successful', commenting that 'the presence of the assistant lent an air of authenticity and realism to the procedings.' Paired work with two language teachers can also be very effective, and some schools even timetable an extra languages teacher in a given year to move as a pair-working resource from class to class.

[3] Kelly (op. cit. p. 13) quotes a direct recommendation of 1531 to use this method in teaching Latin, from Sir Thomas Elyot in *The Boke named the Governour*.

9 Beyond the classroom: language in use

Within the classroom much of what we do must involve suspension of disbelief and deferred gratification. Even when we have proceeded from learning the means of constructing language to genuine communication, it is clear that talking to the teacher, our pairwork partner, or even the French assistant in our limited French is not the most efficient way of communicating a message. We have a highly developed maternal language in which we can do that, a language all our interlocutors can understand, and paradoxically the more genuine and immediate the message to be conveyed, the greater is the reluctance to use the limited second language rather than the efficient first. The language teacher may well read out in French the message brought round cancelling games; she is rather less likely to conduct a fire evacuation in the foreign language!

It is not easy to set up situations in England where the pupil's French is his most efficient resource for communication. None the less it is important to make him continually aware that French is not just something used in the classroom, and to provide situations outside the classroom learning of the language where his French can legitimately and effectively be employed, even if he realizes that English would actually be easier to use.

We have already pointed to the assistant as the most useful resource to bring French reality to the pupils, but most towns also have a vast untapped reservoir of native speakers. Has the assistant met other French people during her stay with us? Are there French parents or grandparents of children in school? Can these be recruited? If the town has a languages club or a town-twinning committee, these too can be explored for living resources. Having found them, it is not very difficult to persuade them to come into school for the occasional visit — the idea of helping English children learn their native language is usually an attractive one. How should we use them? Many of them will be older than the assistant, come from different parts of France, have different interests. They can be used as an object of pupil interrogation as the assistant was, extending the pupils' view of France; but brought into class with the assistant they can add a new dimension: that of comprehension of French conversation in which the English pupil is not taking a major role. The French produced by a French person speaking to an English learner is quite different from that produced when he or she is taking part in a conversation with another French person, even when the English learner is involved in that conversation. Here, with our extra visitor, is an opportunity to practise comprehension of a type of French the learner may very frequently meet in France, in a way that is not otherwise possible. The topic of conversation between assistant and visitor and the main areas within it to be covered need to be predetermined and basic vocabulary work done by the regular teacher with the class in the lesson before this; the teacher needs to note down gist questions as the conversation goes on, limit it to bursts of five minutes or so, work on the gist questions with the class immediately afterwards, go back to the assistant and visitor for elucidation of problem points, then start the conversation rolling again. A period spent in this way is still 'practice for France', but it comes very near in comprehension skills to the real situation.

With small sixth-form groups an efficient and imaginative assistant on her own can break down the classroom wall very simply by taking the pupils walking outside the school, discussing what she and they see, and comparing it with what she (or they) would expect in France. A country lane, a suburban road, the high street, a car-park, a supermarket — here is a realistic way of revisiting a vocabulary area and using the realia that come to hand.[1]

For both fifth and sixth forms a French day, or better, a French weekend, can come very close to reproducing life in France and its language demands, if both the teachers and the assistant (and student teachers, if available), involved refuse to speak anything but French throughout the weekend.[2] Again, the ability to get outside the classroom and outside the school produces a completely new set of realia: making the bed, washing-up, sweeping the common room, preparing a meal, collecting the coffee, and so on, all give realistic opportunities for language use in new, real situations. The one unreal restriction, that English must not be used, is hardly more restricting than it would be in France, given the pupils' ability to paraphrase by this stage and the fact that objects themselves and the linguistic resource — assistant and teachers — are there to hand. Such courses *do* need to be generously staffed, however.

There are other, less intensive ways of giving a taste of life in France within an English context. A well-organized languages club with the assistant heavily involved is one. French films and video-tapes, French board and card games, French pop music and play-readings, cooking a French lunch, making a model of a French town, listening to the assistant talking about and demonstrating her hobby, listening to taped material from the foreign sister-school — all this brings one closer to reality and involves a good deal of passive comprehension of real language and the occasional active use of the language for communication.³ All forms of reading of French, watching French films on television or French video-tapes, listening to French radio, are in fact part of this opening up of the classroom walls, though to be honest these are mostly elements of a sixth-form course, rather than realistic parts of something lower down the school. A French person faced with a foreign learner repeats, rephrases, emphasizes, slows, simplifies: a book or a film of course does not. French reality in printed or taped form is more difficult to cope with than the real French person. It is none the less readily usable in the form of *correspondance sonore*⁴ where the tape has been specially produced with a particular class or individuals in mind and the French pupils, guided by the French teacher, have organized their language for maximum comprehensibility.

A further source of immediate communication in the foreign language may be the paying guest. Especially in German there is demand here, since there is a great imbalance between the number of English pupils learning German and of German pupils learning English. A paying guest in a home where an exchange is not possible may be the next best thing. Clearly the foreign visitor is here to learn English and will wish to speak it most of the time: none the less the occasional hour of German is a relaxation for him and a valuable direct contact in the language for a child of the English host learning German.

Finally in this area of realistic use of the foreign language one must mention the *sections bilingues*, pioneered in this country in Somerset and Hertfordshire and, in the independent sector, at Mill Hill School, where subjects within the normal school timetable are taught in the foreign language.⁵ There are some reservations in that a subject-specific register has to be taught which may not be of much value outside that particular classroom; but beyond this there is a great deal of basic language that is common to all subjects and the necessity in this context of really concentrating on the message (we are not just learning French, we are learning geography too, and that's very important) makes this a genuinely communicative exercise. There are problems of staffing, and of motivation (if you really dislike geography you may very well end up disliking French as well — and vice-versa), but where this approach has been tried the resultant language success has always been attributed to having a content to communicate that is seen by both teachers and learners as essentially non-trivial.

In fact, though, these are all substitutes for the French reality: breaking down the classroom walls and using the language in a real context ultimately means getting our students to the country itself. The simplest visit, the day trip, is by no means a waste of time if properly organized. The day trip to France, given motorways and hovercraft, is a possibility for the majority of the school population of England and Wales. Its value is twofold: it proves to the pupil on the one hand that France exists and that the French language is used by real, normal people for everyday transactions — something that it is difficult to grasp in an other than abstract, intellectual way for many young language learners. It also proves that France is somewhere accessible, right next door to parts of England, real and reachable in the same way that Dover is. This point should not be underestimated: it becomes the more important the further north or west our pupils live.

The second value of the day trip lies in what we make of it in relation to our classroom work. Even if the trip is so early in the course that little more than precise visual observation and comprehension is possible, this itself is of value. Fifty questions can be devised along the lines of: what is the French for toyshop, what sign can you see outside a tobacconist's, what colour are letter-boxes, what is the French for bus-stop, what do the words *autres directions* indicate, what is the cheapest drink on the *boissons pilotes* list outside cafés, what is a motorized bicycle called, what is the colour sequence of French traffic lights, what is a *librairie*, how do you say 'no parking' in French . . . ? With a prize for pupils with fifty correct answers or for the pupil who comes nearest, this exercise demands observation and deduction and will lead, ultimately, to 'why' questions in class after the visit. The necessity of buying lunch and souvenirs involves preparatory units of oral work in food and drink and shopping; finding one's way back to the rendezvous point or (in emergency) the hoverport necessitates a unit on asking and following directions. The compulsion imposed by the visit gives the preparatory work real point; it is no bad idea to give all the work actually done in Boulogne or Calais to pairs rather than individuals and to use the same pairings as are normally involved in class pairwork. The importance of this sort of observation trip ultimately lies in the pupils' increased involvement in France. Simply take them there as a group and they keep their group solidarity — the French are 'them', the group is 'us', the strange world of Calais or Boulogne is kept at a distance, almost like three-dimensional television. But given a precise task, equipped with a town plan, and sent out in groups of not more than two to do it, and this them-us dichotomy breaks. The individual is involved.

This sort of day trip is only really possible with French. Even Aachen is too far for anything less than an overnight stay with its attendant problems and expense, and for Spanish, Italian, or Russian this rapid-day exposure to reality is of course quite impossible. It is a small additional argument for French rather than other languages as the standard language for the language-experience course.

We have already suggested that the ultimate goal of the language-experience course should be a stay in the foreign country, preferably of a week's duration, certainly of several days. By this time, at the end of at least two years, some real ability in oral production should also be there and should be put to the practical test of use in the country. A log of activities to complete is essential for this visit. It is a good idea to specify different tasks each day in the log. Some, such as buying a meal in a café or restaurant, will take place on a number of days, but on the logged day will be treated with special attention. Suitable topics may be: buying a meal; pricing specified articles in a supermarket and comparing their prices with those of similar items in Britain, established before starting the trip; buying postcards, discovering the postal rate to Great Britain and buying stamps; discovering the French for, pricing, and buying, adhesive wound dressings; buying a French comic and recounting one story from it in English; getting from point A to point B by public transport, with a complete account of how this is done including cost; collecting the contents of as many public signs and notices as possible with an English explanation of what each means; and so on. Each day's topics should be disclosed on the morning of that day and the logs collected and marked on the same evening. If sufficient suitable French interlocutors are available, at least one of the topics should involve the conveying and discovery of personal information. It is here that those Local Education Authorities score that have permanent hostels in France and a developed relationship with the local community. An Authority does not of course have to go to the expense of a hostel to produce this: some have established permanent French campsites or taken over parts of *colonies de vacances*.[6]

Apart from the organized visit at the end of the language-experience course, other trips abroad should be encouraged and utilized. A family trip to the Pyrenees, say, known of beforehand, can be used as part of an individual or group project on the southwest, and specific discovery tasks set; pen- and tape-friends can similarly be used to obtain materials for project work; town-twinning schemes too will yield valuable project information from informants prejudiced in favour of enquiries from pupils in the twinned town. Schools in town-twinning schemes and with other school links abroad often send pupils to the continent on trips organized by departments other than the modern languages department, with the school orchestra, sports teams, choir, plays, geography field courses, and so on being the original reason for the trip. Liaison here with the organizing school department and appropriate language preparation can often ensure that the trip also has a positive outcome for the pupil in terms of what he did with his French or German as well as with his oboe.

There is little doubt, however, that at the higher levels of language learning the most productive type of visit is the home-to-home exchange, and we have already advocated this in both Chapter 5 and Chapter 6. Exchange visits can take several different forms.

The simplest form is the two- or three-week person-to-person exchange, usually with a teacher or teachers from the English school in the offing as trouble-shooters and perhaps with a couple of group visits or activities, but basically relying for its value on the host family and the degree of integration of the English pupil within this family. Cultural preparation can be made for this as well as some obvious linguistic preparation, but it is in no way possible to prepare the student linguistically for all the situations (or all the functions) he may need in the course of a three-week stay. The total time spent speaking and listening to French on the exchange visit may well be the equivalent of the whole of the time spent so far in school learning that language.[8] It is therefore important that such an exchange be placed reasonably far into the mastery course so that the pupil is able to generate comprehensible French in any situation and follow what is said to him when it is deliberately expressed. His writing, too, should be at the stage (perfect tense required at least!) where he can keep a daily diary of what he has done, which should then be read and (lightly) corrected by the host family each evening. It is important that the pupil uses the time in the family in a linguistically valuable way, not treating the holiday *merely* as a holiday. Such a diary, though written, helps to reinforce new oral learning. If the French exchange partner has to help in its writing, so much the better!

A variant on the person-to-person exchange, one which takes a great deal more organizing but is felt by many teachers to be of greater value, is the class-to-class exchange. Here the object is a fortnight's intensive class teaching, rather than simply a holiday in a French family. The pupil is still paired with a French partner (in whose home he may or may not be sleeping) and for most of the time they work together as a pair. Alternate days are taught in French and English, with input at the beginning of each session to the whole (double) class from a teacher or teachers of the appropriate nationality; then the pairs take over; within each pair the pupil whose native language is the language of the day takes on the teaching role. At appropriate points pairs can change their composition and the new native speaker in the reconstituted pair now takes on the role of tester, discovering how effectively the non-native has learned with his teaching partner. This pairwork is coupled with work outside in the community related to it of the kind suggested earlier for the language-experience visit. Such work outside the classroom then also serves as part of the input to the next day's pairwork. This sort of class exchange is often felt to provide a more efficient learning structure than the home-to-home exchange.[9] It is true that the latter relies very much more on the degree of sympathy engendered between hosts and guest for its effectiveness and thus is much more hit-and-miss. At its best, however, it does present the complete survive-and-grow situation which the class exchange does not quite offer.

At a sixth-form level the short exchange can be linked directly to a civilization project of some depth and if the host family are aware what this is to be before the exchange takes place they can usually be extremely helpful, not just in providing access to materials but in arranging interviews with people useful as informants for the English student. At a sixth-form level term exchanges are also possible, either on an individual student basis or on a full-class basis. A number of schools now organize the latter as a half-term exchange in the lower-sixth year, with the lower-sixth linguists spending six weeks in the foreign school and their counterparts returning with them to spend the other half of the term in England. These longer exchanges involve considerable problems of administration, and it is quite vital for the parents of the pupils paired to get to know each other through extensive correspondence well before these lengthier exchanges take place. The class exchanges at this level do of course have the advantage that, at any rate in the language lessons, more specifically appropriate work can be organized than with individual exchanges, where the exchangee has to be treated to all intents and purposes as a normal member of the foreign school's sixth form — something which has both advantages and disadvantages.

Finally, in opening up areas where the student can and must actually use his or her language, the possibility of working abroad must not be discounted. Even in difficult economic times short-term jobs still exist in areas such as the catering trade or working as *moniteurs* in *colonies de vacances*, and pupils over the age of 18 at the end of their course can find such a realistic taste of the world of work in the foreign country rewarding linguistically as well as financially.[10]

Finally, how can we as teachers use the time the student spends in the foreign country to test what has been taught, to see whether our teaching has been effective? It is important, as can be seen from the foregoing, to give the pupils structured tasks to accomplish in the foreign country wherever possible (and it almost always *is* possible with a little thought), from simple observation at the lowest level to interviewing and collecting of materials to produce a project of some intellectual content at the highest. It is by monitoring the effectiveness with which these tasks have been carried out that we can, at any rate in part, assess the effectiveness of our teaching in preparation for the foreign adventure. If most pupils answer the French question quiz, or produce logs showing the successful undertaking of the daily task set, or come back from their family exchange with a lengthy and interesting diary in French, or produce a sixth-form project of real depth, then we are entitled to assume some effectiveness in the sort of teaching we have been providing. But this is really no more than a sampling of what was going on. We have used, earlier in this paragraph, the word 'adventure' for the first time in this book. That is really what the end-product of this language learning is or should be, an adventure, exciting and unpredictable. And because it is unpredictable, it is ultimately untestable by the teacher in any predetermined way. However, for the pupil, at each moment of the adventure, the direst test exists. It is: did I understand what he or she said? Could I reply what I wanted to reply? Did they understand what I said? The test, always, for the pupil, is effective communication. That is what, as we have stressed throughout this book, language learning is for.

Footnotes

[1] The words 'efficient' and 'imaginative' at the head of this paragraph are important. In the author's experience this device works extremely well, but only where the assistant is authoritative and quick-thinking.

² We have already indicated the place of such a weekend in a sixth-form course in Chapter 6. See chapter 6, footnote 9.

³ At a sixth-form level the Institut Français (or its equivalents in other languages) can be of great value for those within easy reach of 15 Queensbury Place, South Kensington. It provides, from time to time, theatre, art exhibitions, films, talks, a library, and, of course, a highly French atmosphere.

⁴ Again, we have already referred to the place of this, in Chapter 4. See p. 71.

⁵ For a fuller account see King A. 'Haygrove Comprehensive School' in Hawkins E. W. and Perren G. (eds.) *Intensive Language Teaching in Schools* CILT 1978.

⁶ Details of these and other useful travel information are to be found in *School Travel and Exchange*, published by the Central Bureau for Educational Visits and Exchanges.

⁷ For all types of exchange visit, the Central Bureau for Educational Visits and Exchanges, Seymour Mews House, Seymour Mews, Wigmore Street, London W1H 0AA, are enormously helpful. They are the first people to approach in setting up a new exchange.

⁸ Three weeks, sixteen hours a day, is 336 hours. Four years, two hours a week, is 318 hours.

⁹ A typical class-exchange of this kind is described by Race A. T. and Thorpe J. in 'Exchange groups and pair work' in *The Teaching of Modern Languages* (op. cit.) p. 45. Hawkins describes similar courses mounted in York (Hawkins E. *Modern Languages in the Curriculum* Cambridge University Press 1981 p. 193).

¹⁰ The *Service culturel* of the French Embassy (22 Wilton Crescent, London SW1X 8SB) may be able to help here, and the annual publication *Emplois d'Été en France* (Vac-Job, 4 rue d'Alésia, 75014 Paris) is also invaluable for specific summer jobs in France. The Central Bureau and the National Union of Students (3 Endsleigh Street, London WC1) are also helpful.

10 To sum up

In *The School Curriculum* (HMSO, 1981) the Secretary of State for Education and the Secretary of State for Wales considered what might be the appropriate curricular provision for modern languages in secondary schools and recommended that most pupils should have the opportunity to learn a language, with two, or preferably three, years as the minimum provision. Pupils should also, it was considered, be encouraged to continue to learn a language until the end of the fifth year, where possible.

Whilst this book was being written the consultative paper that resulted from this was published.[1] It lists a number of major issues of language-teaching policy to be decided nationally, and it may be interesting to consider these issues in the light of the organization and content of modern languages studies proposed in the present work. The issues concern, the paper suggests:

- the case for all pupils beginning to learn a foreign language at age 11;
- the possible postponement of the start of foreign language learning for some pupils to age 12, 13, or 14;
- the means of identifying those, if any, for whom foreign-language learning is not appropriate;
- the design of courses for lower-attaining pupils of lasting value and benefit;
- the resource and other implications of differentiated provision for different groups of pupils.[2]

Taking these points in order:

1 The case for all pupils having a coherent experience of a foreign language has been made in Chapter 1 and Chapter 3. The experience of the Primary French experiment shows that generally this is best kept for the secondary school and the logical place for it is at or towards the beginning of the secondary course.

2 The later start to foreign language learning and the more intensive course that would result from this has its attractions: on our scheme *all* pupils choosing to learn a foreign language for mastery would start later, preferably at 13. But they would start with

a self-contained language-experience course behind them and with acquired language-learning skills.

3 By age 13 pupils themselves identify whether a course is appropriate or not. Often they do this on quite inadequate evidence. On the basis of the language-experience course, however, they have two years of language learning to base this decision on. With efficient, effective, imaginative work on that course more pupils will make the voluntary choice to continue language learning for mastery. And of course the fact that they are volunteers rather than conscripts will make them readier to learn and more rewarding to teach.

4 The language-experience course does not need to be simply a course for lower-attaining pupils. It is different in kind from the language-mastery course and of value to all. It is topic based and teaching it to a wide ability range presents no insuperable problems. The language-mastery course can, naturally, be setted by ability if there is sufficient demand in the school, and pace and methods suitably adjusted to the different groups. But generally speaking, all, including lower-attaining pupils, should benefit from the language-experience course, and linguistically gifted children should then be encouraged to forge ahead on the mastery course.

5 The implications for the type of differentiation we propose are mainly to do with teaching methods and materials — the approaches to language experience and language mastery are, as we have seen, very different, since aims are quite different. But generally an awareness of language as communication, which is at the root of both courses, implies availability of financial resources to enable pupils to spend organized time in the country whose language they are learning, as a necessary part of their course, not as an optional extra. It is here (and probably only here) that additional resources may be needed. Much though depends on an LEA's existing attitude to time spent abroad and how far it already makes provision for some form of support for this.

What then, in sum, have we been advocating in this book in terms of organization and objectives? Much of what we have suggested is possible within the old-fashioned framework of a five-year course from age 11; all of it could be implemented with the very minimum of disruption to the standard school curriculum with options at 13 or 14. It does mean, though, for many individual teachers and often for whole departments, a change of viewpoints as to what language teaching is *for*, and the ability to see that different language courses may legitimately have quite different aims.

We start, as the DES does, from the idea that the foreign language learning experience should be part of the curriculum for virtually all children, and that the best time to provide this in terms of available resources is at age 11.³ If this experience is valuable for all it should form a coherent and self-contained unit in the curriculum. Failing to complete a five-year course does not provide this. Therefore the first two or three years of modern language learning (our own preference is for a two-year course) should be organized in a self-contained way to show pupils how languages work and to give them experience in the basics of one language, leaving them with a limited but usable resource. Viewing the first two years in this way enables them to be treated as self-contained and different from the later specialist course.⁴ A whole range of practical considerations (including the accessibility of the country) means that the language of this course should normally be French.⁵ Such a course, taught on the basis of topic areas and functions and with use of the language in the country built in as an end-objective, can be taught to a wide ability range, with mixed-ability teaching possible though not necessary.

Subsequent to this a mastery course or courses should be on offer. These, taught *ab initio* and on a linear basis would offer the widest range of languages possible compatible with a three-year course leading to (or rather, taking in) the examinations at 16+. It should be possible here to widen the range of languages taught, and to include ethnic languages to a much greater extent than is at present possible.⁶ German and Spanish could be offered instead of, or in larger schools as alternatives to, French as the first linear language without the concern (often expressed by parents) that the child has thereby no knowledge of French at all. In larger schools where qualified staff are available it should be possible to arrange the timetable so that children with a linguistic bent could opt for two mastery courses in different languages.

The reorganization of sixth-form teaching to offer a self-contained first-year language course, keeping literature to form a central part of the second-year course, would help meet the objection that students at 16+ are often offered an unsuitable grammar-translation and literature course or nothing.⁷ It would also enable schools to change more readily to the new language-based A levels if and when they wished to.

These are the major organizational changes that this book proposes. None of them is impractical or revolutionary, and all of them can be found functioning efficiently in schools somewhere;

some of them have been doing so for many years. What of our proposals for course content?

Here, throughout the book, we have been insisting on communication as our aim, a genuine aim, built into the course and tested, rather than a pious hope. All our methodological suggestions have been made with this ultimate end in view. At lower levels, especially within the language-experience course, this may mean preparing the pupil to use his language in a limited range of situations and with only functional accuracy; at higher levels our course must include mastery of all useful forms. In both cases language learning must lead to language use, at the everyday classroom level in a simulation of reality, at the culminating point or points of the course in actual use of the language for specific ends in the country. Hence our stress on pairwork practice and the paramount importance of fluency, be it in aural comprehension, extensive reading, or oral production. Throughout our teaching we must be seen to be leading our pupils to autonomous use of the language, and at the ultimate stage of the learning process to a concentration on what they want to express rather than on the means of expression. This in turn means providing situations in which the learner has an overwhelming need and demand to express himself in the foreign language, a compulsion to communicate. We have expressed scepticism about the appropriateness of most available examinations to test a course with such aims, whilst viewing many of the schemes of graded objectives and tests with some enthusiasm.

Finally we have introduced the idea of adventure, and in sum this is what language learning should be — a gateway to adventure, an opening out of our pupils' lives, an enlargement of their personal possibilities and potential. This will not be achieved through learning the rules governing the agreement of the past participle with the preceding direct object with *avoir* verbs; it may, just, by keeping in the forefront of the mind at all times the idea that travelling to the foreign country and functioning effectively when we get there is what we are learning the language for, that what we are getting is a skill, which, when we meet our counterparts in France and Germany, in Belgium and Spain, in Austria and Italy and Russia, will help humanize our view of them and theirs of us by understanding and communication.

Footnotes

[1] *Foreign Languages in the school curriculum* DES and Welsh Office 1983.

[2] Ibid. p. 7.

[3] 'The case for a later [i.e. secondary] start on language learning for most pupils is based . . . on practical considerations. The limited specialist resources are better deployed at the secondary stage.' Ibid. p. 6.

[4] 'For most pupils their three years' experience [as at present constituted] is not designed to be self-contained and does not therefore give most of them a usable competence.' Ibid. p. 7.

[5] Not the least of these is staffing. Though there is unused capacity in available teaching strength in the minority languages, it is quite peripheral in relation to the numbers of French teachers available. Only one languages teacher in five in our schools is qualified to teach German, one in 12 to teach Spanish, one in 23 Italian, one in 35 Russian (Figures based on Secondary Schools Staffing Survey, November 1977). No large-scale move away from French as the first language experienced by most of our children is possible.

[6] Only modern Chinese, with about the same number of O-level entries as Russian, is currently taught at all widely to examination level, if O-level entries are any guide. Within the framework suggested it would be much easier to offer such languages as equal alternatives to the major European languages.

[7] 'It is arguable that at least those sixth formers who have achieved a higher grade result in a foreign language at O-level or CSE should continue to learn that language (or another) whether or not they intend to offer it for A-level.' *Foreign Languages in the school curriculum* (op. cit.) p. 9.

Bibliographical note

There is little point in appending a list of titles for further reading and addresses for reference when the Centre for Information on Language Teaching and Research has already done this so splendidly. Among their bibliographical guides I would single out

    Teaching Modern Languages 1979
    Language Teaching Methodology 1980
    Teaching Materials for French 1980; supplement 1982
    Teaching Materials for German/Italian/Russian/Spanish (all 1983)

and the invaluable

    CILT Directory of Organizations and Centres for Language Teachers and Students 1981.

The current CILT publications catalogue is available from 20 Carlton House Terrace, London SW1Y 5AP, and CILT answers telephone queries readily, quickly, politely, and helpfully, on 01 839 2626.